A SUCCESSFUL LIFE

A SUCCESSFUL LIFE

FINDING SUCCESS WHILE CREATING HAPPINESS

By

GABRIEL LAWSON

*i*Odyssey Books
the intelligent journey

Copyright

Published by iOdyssey LLC
Monument, CO 80132

Print Edition 2011: 10 9 8 7 6 5 4 3
    ISBN-13: 978-0-9827642-0-6
    ISBN-10: 0982764200
ePub Edition 2011
    ISBN-13: 978-0-9827642-1-3
    ISBN-10: 0982764219

About the Publisher:
United States
iOdyssey LLC
19153 Strawberry Lane
Monument, CO 80132
http://www.iodyssey.net

Dedication

To my wife and best friend, whose support and love keeps me always going forward.

Contents

Introduction

If you had better problem solving skills, more creativity, and enhanced intuitive abilities, along with better health, enhanced personal interaction, and improved emotional skills, do you feel you would be more successful in your professional and personal life? Maybe I should ask, is there any way you could imagine NOT being more successful given your new-found advantages?

You can embrace these advantages and permit abundance to flow more freely into your career and your private life. The key to embracing abundance is *entrainment*—a scientific term originally coined in the 17th century that is regaining popularity due to startling recent scientific discoveries. If you have not heard of entrainment, you are not alone. I had no knowledge of the term or of how it could change my life until I became a volunteer at a hospice in January of 1997.

I went to help the dying as they prepared to leave behind lifetimes filled with joys, hardships, families, friends, and careers. As a volunteer, I was merely another person who could make beds, wash faces, feed patients, help change diapers, and, whenever I had the time, to visit and listen. In small ways, I helped these strangers-turned-friends as they exhausted the remaining days of their lives. Yet, I wasn't doing the majority of helping; it was they who were helping me. Time after time, I found myself the recipient of their smiles, their stories, their advice, and their wisdom. I found people did all sorts of things to earn a living. I found there were other things of which they were more proud. I also found some secrets. Of most significance was what they said was the most important thing in life.

Realizing that one day I too would look back and judge the success or failure of my life—as my new friends were doing as they faced death—I decided to make some bold changes in my approach to work and life regardless of the consequences I was certain to encounter. Believing these changes would limit my success in my career, I was amazed to find the opposite. In reality, success became easier.

Imagine my surprise when in a relatively short time I went from the position of manager to director, then to vice president, and then to senior vice president in high tech corporate America. My income more than doubled in this short time span! I certainly didn't understand how this could happen. However, with dedication, hard work, and some luck, I uncovered a number of unrelated new scientific discoveries in various social, biological and physical sciences that explained why these simple strategies derived from the secrets of the dying worked. New scientific discoveries prove that by following some simple guidelines, the human body and mind function at optimal levels. We actually shift the odds of success in our favor.

An Example of Entrainment

On its surface, entrainment appears to be as unscientific as luck. It is not. There is hard science behind how entrainment works. You can easily create the conditions necessary for entrainment to occur in your life.

In his best-selling book *Men are From Mars, Women are from Venus*, John Gray describes a situation that illustrates the concept of entrainment. John was working very hard to be successful in his career. He assumed professional success meant he could provide the material things that would allow both himself and his wife to be happy. John wanted to be a good provider. The harder he worked to create a better life for his wife and family, the more his marriage and his work seemed to struggle. Finally, he decided a new course of action was required. John's busy schedule consisted of seeing eight clients daily. He decreased his work schedule to seven clients daily and reallocated the eighth client's hour to his wife. For one hour each day he gave his wife the undivided attention he gave each of his clients. His plan worked miracles for his relationship with his wife and family. John's plan to sacrifice his professional career for the sake of his family paid huge dividends in his personal life: he and his wife enjoyed renewed happiness while his work—well, somehow his work thrived. He was enjoying more success in his professional work, yet he was actually working less.[1]

By focusing on his wife and their relationship, John Gray became more successful. So what happened? He worked less and became more successful while also achieving his goal of a better relationship with his wife. Was this luck?

3

No, it was not luck! John had unknowingly applied some of the principles of entrainment to his life. As a result, he had stumbled upon the secret of the ancient Eastern concept of "do less and accomplish more."

Do not assume from this brief example that the secret to entrainment is not caring about your work. Caring is a critical element in living a successful life. A successful life is much more than just being successful in your career. It is about being successful in both your life and your work.

Joyful Living

Life would be much easier if we won the lottery—or would it? Recent studies show most lottery winners are no happier six months after they win the lottery than before they won. How could this be possible? It is possible because success is more than outward abundance. Inward happiness forms the other face of the two-sided coin we know as success. Thus, a successful life means success in many aspects of our lives: our emotions, our physical health, our spiritual life, and our material world.

Major misconceptions about success arise from the material world. Continually confronting us and seeking center stage in our assessment of the success of our lives, the material world creates an image of success in our minds, and we work for it, dream of it and wait for it to appear. Once realized, however, our happiness rarely changes. We may have achieved the new house, automobile, boat or whatever material thing that composed our image of success. However, we are rarely happier.

A recent study indicates that in creating happiness, money rates near the bottom.[2] Yet we remain enslaved to a material lifestyle that doesn't allow us to fully experience and enjoy life. We obtain our material quests, only to set off quickly in pursuit of another one. This one, we are sure, will make us happy, but it doesn't. We experience moments of exhilaration and happiness, but most of the time we are not fully satisfied with our lives.

We put tremendous effort towards our objectives (be it our work or our personal lives). We sacrifice our personal time so we can climb the corporate ladder, make our own business succeed, or chase the latest carrot dangling in front of our noses. Too often, we place our goals and objectives ahead of people. We sacrifice spending time with the special people in our lives: our families, our children, our girlfriend or boyfriend or our friends. We are willing to sacrifice a lot that we value to get ahead, but this is not success. If we sacrifice one thing of value for another thing of value, then we have not succeeded—*we have simply made a trade.*

Yet, there is another way, one that has brought more abundance in my life than I ever thought possible. It comes without sacrificing one thing we value for something else we believe will make us happy. A successful life arises when we optimize our skills so they work in harmony with one another. When we place our emotional, intellectual, physical, and spiritual realms in harmony with one another, we create a state of quantum synchronicity. A successful life means achieving abundance and happiness in work, in family, and in play—that is, in everything we do—without sacrificing those things we value.

New science shows us how we can increase our problem solving abilities, decision making skills, creativity, intuition, emotional intelligence and physical health. When optimized, these elements work in a state of harmony known as *entrainment*. This entrainment factor is powerful. Its application is simple and it does not compromise those things we hold dear in life. It enriches and brings happiness and abundance.

What You Will Learn

Lao Tsu, the recognized author of the Tao Te Ching—the 2,500-year-old ancient Taoist text translated more often than any book except the Bible—wrote that the essence of his teaching was, 'a violent man dies a violent death.'[3]

The Golden Rule and the concept that you reap what you sow is the essence of Jesus' teachings. I am amazed at the similarities found in the essence of our great religious teachers: Jesus, Buddha, Muhammad, Lao Tsu. Each speaks of the importance of how we treat one another and that what we do determines what we experience. Joining our great religious prophets, our quantum physicists are expounding the principle that we have much more of an impact on the world around us than we might think. The discovery of the "uncertainty principle" by the German physicist Werner Heisenberg, allowed our physicists to conclude that the act of observing an experiment influences the outcome.[4]

Heisenberg's Law of Uncertainty proved that an independent, neutral observer does not exist. We change the outcome of an experiment by simply observing it. We (and everything) are interconnected.

This interconnectivity opens up and enhances our natural abilities once we understand the basics of how our mind, our body, and the external world actually work. New discoveries by our scientific community in the social, biological and physical sciences greatly enhance our chances of being successful in all aspects of our lives once we understand how easy it is to apply them.

This book teaches what it means to be successful from a life perspective. Life is the foundation on which all activities rest; thus, it is the primary focus of this book. You will learn the meaning of life as seen through people who are facing death. You will learn the meaning of life as seen through the eyes of people who died and returned to life—the near-death experience. The five steps presented in this book reveal how to live a successful life, but you can apply these steps to any aspect of life, whether it is in your professional career or your personal life. I have included at the end of each of the five steps a section on how to apply the life concepts to any activity you undertake.

* * *

To help understand entrainment, Thomas Cleary tells an old Chinese story in his translation of *The Art of War*, an ancient Chinese text regularly studied in corporate America for its guidance on business strategy and philosophy. The story is about a Chinese emperor who, upon learning that his medical physician came from a family of three healers, asks who the better physician was.

The physician told the emperor that his eldest brother removes sickness when it is still spirit. As a result, his name is not heard outside the house.

The elder brother sees sickness while it is small, so he is known only in the neighborhood.

I massage skin and give herbs after sickness is easily recognized. Hence, I am widely known among the poor and the rich.[5]

This story depicts three success methods. The brother that massages skin and prescribes herbs parallels the concept of hard work, which was the prevalent theory and practice of the early and middle part of the 20th century. Our parents worked hard for the companies that employed them and were rewarded with the security of working for one company their entire lives before retirement. However, working hard at something is not always the most efficient or effective way of achieving our goals.

Working hard had been the default method that most people and managers turn to when facing looming deadlines. Henry Ford, a pioneer in productivity studies, showed that working five days per week produced the same amount of work as working six days per week. Thus, he created the 40-hour workweek.[6]

A hundred years of productivity studies confirm Ford's results. For both physically intensive jobs and knowledge workers, productivity drops over time when working more than 40 hours per week. Less than 40 hours per week also produces less than 40 hours of productivity. In 1908, Ernst Abbe was the first to show an increase in daily output by reducing the daily work schedules from nine to eight hours per day.[7]

Due to the phenomenon known as the "fatigue factor" studies show that initial productivity rises when initiating overtime, but quickly starts to decline. For example, an eight-week 60-hour workweek will show an initial productivity increase. By week four, the average productivity falls to only 40 hours per week and continues to decline each week thereafter. By week eight, the loss in productivity during the last 4 weeks cancels out the first four weeks' productivity gains. Eight weeks at 60 hours yields an overall average of 40 hours of productivity per week.[8] Extending a 60-hour workweek to 12 weeks yields an average productivity of only 19.5 hours per week.

Our minds cannot comprehend that working 30 hours per week for six months (even though this is 10 hours per week below optimum productivity) is far more productive than working 60 hours per week for six months. Getting an "A" for effort, but failing, is far more soothing to our "work hard" conditioning than going against conventional wisdom and finding a better way to be successful.

* * *

The middle brother, who cures sickness while it is small, corresponds to today's mantra of work smart, not hard. This brother is more efficient than the youngest brother; he figured out a faster way to accomplish the same amount of work. Working smart is a better, more efficient method than working hard.

I love to work with my hands, so I tend to do numerous home-improvement projects. Whether it is putting in a new floor, laying tile, putting up a wall, or installing doors, it usually takes me a little while to figure out the best method to do the job. Once I figure it out, I can repeat the process with speed and accuracy. This is efficiency. Doing something efficiently means doing it as quickly as possible. If a manufacturing plant can build 100 parts per hour, increasing efficiency means building 120 parts per hour.

Suppose carpenters can install 20 sq. feet of floor per hour, but at this rate the entire office building installation will take longer than scheduled. The first option that comes to mind is to schedule overtime: work harder. However, suppose that by changing to a wider board for the flooring, the same carpenters can now install 30 sq. feet of floor per hour and finish the job in the allocated time. This is efficiency and is often the second choice behind working harder.

Yet there remains a more effective technique, as illustrated by the eldest brother, which is doing less and accomplishing more. Many gains are realized when one shifts his or her perspective from working hard to working smart. Exponential gain awaits those who can shift their perspectives from working smart to doing less and accomplishing more.

Examine the difference between efficiency and effectiveness. *Efficiency* means doing something faster. *Effectiveness*, however, is different from efficiency. Suppose the flooring installed in the office building does not stand up to the daily grind of thousands of workers in the various offices. Within a year, the building floors are scratched and worn and in need of replacement. With a significant cost to replace the floors, the overall impact to the developer is a loss. While the developer was *efficient* in putting in the original floor, he was not *effective*, as the overall cost of replacing the floor now exceeds the proposed cost and wipes out the original profit. In this case, the developer was *efficient* because he found a faster way to install the flooring, but he was not *effective* because he installed the wrong flooring to meet the demands of the office building. Being *efficient* meant going faster to meet schedule, but being *effective* meant picking the right product to meet the needs of the building.

Picking the right flooring product, in this case, was more important than being efficient in the flooring installation. This principle is what we find in the eldest brother, who removes sickness when it is still spirit. Effectiveness means doing the right thing and doing it once.

As children, the way we play a game matters more than its outcome, but as adults, the final score is all that matters. Our Western way tries to control the outcome: the external, the outside, the observable, the obvious—what I like to call the *consequences*. For example, when undergoing triple bypass surgery for clogged arteries or chemotherapy for lung cancer, we focus on the outcome, not its prevention, similar to the last of our three Chinese physicians:

> I massage skin and give herbs after sickness is easily recognized. Hence, I am widely known among the poor and the rich.

Fighting fires, a daily activity in corporate America, requires employees to work long hours and spend weekends away from their families to extinguish the daily emergencies, only to scurry off to the next fire as soon as the current one is under control. This model says a good manager is one who successfully directs his or her employees in how to handle these fires. A good manager appears to be one who can control the *consequences.*

Corporate America, and our society, rewards this type of behavior. Shouted from rooftop to rooftop are the names of hard-working employees who get the fires under control. Our newscasts rarely broadcast stories of those who prevent fires; quite the opposite is true. Our newscasts show the fires, the accidents, the tragedies, and those men and women who perform heroic acts when called upon.

Yet someone is starting these fires, so find the arsonist! Someone's *behavior* is causing other people to spend tremendous amounts of time putting out those fires. In the corporate world, in many cases, the firefighter and the arsonist are the same! A better manager will search out the arsonist rather than spend his or her energy scattered among a thousand and one fires.

Behind consequences, we find some type of *behavior* causing the *consequences.* If we change the behavior, we can change a thousand and one consequences. It is better to find sickness when it is small, like the second of our Chinese physicians:

> The elder brother sees sickness while it is small, so he is known only in the neighborhood.

A loving person behaves in a loving manner, a defiant person behaves in a defiant manner, and an angry person behaves in an angry manner. This is the essence of Lao Tsu's teaching that a violent man dies a violent death.[9]

What is it that makes someone commit acts of violence, anger, defiance, or love? *Attitude* determines *behavior*. Having love in your heart results in a loving behavior pattern, whereas having defiance in your heart results in a defiant behavior pattern. A violent attitude results in violent behavior. It is best to find the spirit of sickness or the spirit of success before it takes shape, as the first of our three Chinese physicians did:

> The eldest brother removes sickness when it is still spirit. As a result, his name is not heard outside the house.

Our attitude reflects the spirit of sickness or the spirit of wellness. Our *attitude* determines the *behavior* that causes the *consequences*.

When the consequences are not desirable, do not try fixing the consequences. Look for the behavior causing the consequences. Changing the behavior is much easier than trying to change the consequences. Having found the behavior, look for the attitude causing the behavior. Changing an attitude is more efficient and effective than trying to change multiple behaviors.

Our *attitude* determines the *behavior* that causes the *consequences*. I call this philosophy the "successful living ABCs".

ATTITUDE
The eldest brother removes sickness when it is still spirit. As a result, his name is not heard outside the house.

BEHAVIOR
The elder brother sees sickness while it is small, so he is known only in the neighborhood.

CONSEQUENCES
I massage skin and give herbs after sickness is easily recognized. Hence, I am widely known among the poor and the rich.

Our greatest benefits come from modifying attitudes, lesser benefits come from modifying behavior, and the least benefits come from modifying consequences. As mentioned earlier, the perspective we learned as children differs from our adult perspective. The game is different and so are the attitudes, the behaviors, and the consequences. A career in corporate America taught me one set of attitudes, behaviors and consequences. Listening to dying hospice patients as they told me what really is important in life revealed new attitudes, behaviors and consequences that changed my approach to both my work and my life. This led me to discover the secrets of entrainment.

Based on proven scientific discoveries that explain how and why the entrainment factor works, this book explores the right attitudes, behaviors and consequences needed to apply entrainment to help you live a successful life. These "Successful Living ABCs" provide a framework for examining the various elements of and the science behind the entrainment factor.

The three major parts of this book provide an understanding of entrainment and its application in our lives:

- Part 1 examines entrainment and the benefits it brings to our lives.

- Part 2 provides guidelines to assist in applying entrainment to our personal and professional lives.

- Part 3 reveals the secret behind why entrainment works.

As we learn how the entrainment factor can create a successful life, we will explore five principles that summarize characteristics of entrained individuals and entrained groups (teams, corporations, etc.). I present each of the five principles found in the three parts of this book from three perspectives:

- First, a short story illustrates one or more key points of the principle.

- Next, we learn about the principle by exploring various views and scientific evidence that relate to it.

- Lastly, we dive down into the practical applications of the principle, showing how consistently applying the principle can help create success in all aspects of our lives, both large and small.

PART 1: WHAT IS ENTRAINMENT?

Section 1 - Purpose

"Some day, after we have mastered the winds, the waves, the tides and gravity...we shall harness... the energies of love. Then for the second time in the history of the world, man will have discovered fire."

Teilhard de Chardin

Thomas Edison once said, "genius is one percent inspiration, ninety-nine percent perspiration."[10] Part 1's first section reveals the inspiration or catalyst behind my discovery of the key to successful living. Part 1's second section examines new scientific discoveries that show what entrainment is and how it works.

Within the inspiration of this first section of Part 1, we find the first step and key ingredient to creating a successful life: purpose.

Purpose: A Story

Once, three spiritual seekers decided to accelerate their path to enlightenment, so they embarked upon a spiritual pilgrimage. One of the three, Naojo, hearing of a holy man rumored to live in the mountains far to the East, suggested they seek out the holy one. The other two, Knarfi and Namder, agreed this would be a wise path to follow. Surely, a holy one could show them the way to enlightenment that had thus far eluded them.

On the 31st day of their journey, they came upon a campsite. A figure clothed in a full red robe, with a hood drawn upon its head, sat facing a small glowing fire. Naojo, Knarfi, and Namder could not see a face as they approached from the rear. As they drew near, the figure spoke without turning to face them.

"Good evening," the figure said in a gentle voice.

All were startled, as the road they traveled was hard and they had made little or no noise as they approached.

Naojo, still somewhat shocked, somehow managed to reply, "Good evening, sir."

No reply came from the robed stranger. They continued toward the figure, and as they were almost upon him, the figure stated in a low and gentle voice, "Come sit, I have been expecting you. You should have been here yesterday."

The day before, the three had rested by a beautiful lake and did not travel. As the three joined the figure around the fire, the stranger held a steadfast gaze towards the ground, preventing them from seeing his face.

"Enlightenment is a long and hard road. Why do you think you can rest on your journey?" the figure asked.

"Are you the holy one?" inquired Naojo.

"I am no more holy than you. I know of your journey and the holy one sent me to meet and guide you to him," stated the figure, still looking downward.

Continuing, the stranger spoke, "You have chosen a noble path. It is still a long journey to the Master. The path can be very confusing and one can easily lose his way. I will guide you to him, but you must trust me and follow my direction precisely. Is that understood?"

The three men nodded, indicating agreement.

"Good," the figure whispered. "You must sleep now for you will need all your energy for tomorrow."

Morning came and as they awoke, they saw the figure standing some twenty paces up the path with his back to them. They had yet to see the face of this stranger who would take them to enlightenment. The figure waved his arm, motioning them to come. Their journey had finally begun.

They walked briskly. All believed they were of good health, yet it was all they could do to keep up with the figure in the red robe. After traveling all morning, without a break for breakfast or lunch, the figure in the red robe suddenly stopped and, holding up an arm, motioned for all to stop. A loud noise, the sound of an animal crying, came from nearby.

"What was that?" Naojo asked.

At this, the figure turned around and for the first time the men could see the face. The stranger slowly lifted his hands, almost hesitantly, and removed the hood, letting it fall gently onto the shoulders. Long blond hair flowed downward, revealing the face and beauty of a young woman.

"It is a sign from the Master that we are on the right path," the woman revealed.

Overcoming the surprise of the unexpected revelation, Naojo asked, "But what was it?"

"Come," she replied, and they began a side journey towards the direction from where the sound emanated. They soon came upon a huge white bear that had fallen down a cliff and landed on a large flat rock.

"It is a wounded animal," Namder exclaimed.

"This animal has been generous enough to give its life so we may be assured of our way," the young woman said.

"But ... but I thought you knew the way," Naojo replied.

"I do—mostly, but I took a turn a ways back that led me into unfamiliar territory," she stated.

"So, you were lost?" Naojo inquired.

"We are on the right path. We may proceed now. Come, we have to hurry to join the Master before he moves to a new camp," came the reply from the red robed woman.

"Wait!" Naojo interrupted. "You mean the holy one doesn't stay in one place?"

"No, the holy one moves quite often. Now come, hurry. If we don't get there before the moon becomes full again, we will find only a deserted campsite."

"Then, if we are to find our enlightenment, let us go," Naojo stated as if all was now settled.

"WAIT!" Knarfi shouted. "We cannot leave this great white bear to die. There are many bears in this land, but never has anyone seen or heard of a white bear in these parts."

"There is nothing you can do," Naojo responded. "Even so, it would kill you if you tried to approach it."

"Actually, the bear can be saved," the young woman responded. "There is water nearby and plenty of nourishment in the area. The great white bear will not harm you while it is hurt. One of you could stay and nourish it back to health. But," she added, "you will not travel with us to meet the holy one."

"Then it is settled," Naojo interjected. "Let us proceed to meet the holy one."

"No!" Knarfi exclaimed. "I will stay."

"Are you crazy?" Naojo exclaimed.

"Yes," added Namder, "even if it is a white bear, it is still only an animal. There is only the one holy man we know of, and only this opportunity to find him. Surely you will not give up your opportunity to find enlightenment?"

"We have no time to discuss this," the red-robed woman said. "Do you stay or do you go?"

"I stay," Knarfi stated. "My head seeks enlightenment, but my heart is clear. I must stay."

Knarfi did stay. He brought the great white bear nourishment and for six weeks, he took care of the great animal. As time passed, Knarfi wondered about his friends—if they were now enlightened beings. He had so desired enlightenment, yet knew he must wait and attend to the bear.

During the six weeks, Knarfi realized the red-robed woman was right. The bear had been willing to give its life for them. Over time, Knarfi formed a bond with the white bear. He believed the bear was bringing him a message of some sort, a message from the very consciousness of the universe—one that somehow treats death as highly as we treat life.

As Knarfi sat by the fire one night—while the bear lay next to him—the fire, on its own, became much brighter. For the first time, the great white bear stood on its hind legs towering over Knarfi. Also for the first time, Knarfi became afraid. The power of this animal was overwhelming. He was afraid the animal was turning on him—that it would attack and Knarfi's life would be over. As suddenly as the fear came, calmness descended upon Knarfi. He remembered how the spirit of the great white bear had been willing to surrender its life for him and his friends, so they might find enlightenment. If the great white bear had been willing to give its life

24

for him, then Knarfi was willing to give his to the great white bear.

He closed his eyes for one brief moment, awaiting his fate. He reopened them, and standing before him, where the bear had been, was the woman in the red robe.

"You!" Knarfi blurted out. "The bear ... where?"

"Silence," the robed figure whispered. "The Master has left and I am here now." Pausing briefly, she continued. "You gave up your opportunity to find enlightenment. By doing so, you have found it."

Pausing again, giving Knarfi a chance to comprehend, she continued. "Before, when you chose from your heart, when you chose love ahead of your desire for enlightenment, ahead of all else, you chose God's will, your true will, your true nature. It, life, is that simple when you desire that which you truly are and not what you think you should be. You did not realize it, but your greatest desire was love, not enlightenment, and so you now know enlightenment. However, you do have one task you must do before you rejoin the holy one and fully understand. Lower your head, close your eyes, and wait. You must show someone how to choose from the heart as you did. You will know when the time is right."

Knarfi lowered his head as the woman instructed. He waited and after a while realized the woman was gone. He felt a warmth and oneness with her and decided to honor her. With his head still lowered and his eyes still closed, the word "goodbye" formed on his tongue. As he spoke, the word came out in a strange way. He said "Good evening" in a low and gentle voice. Knarfi was puzzled, not so much by the slip of the tongue, but by how his voice sounded—different, softer, and gentler.

"Good evening, kind sir," replied a familiar voice, but Knarfi barely heard or comprehended the other voice. Knarfi, transfixed on the change in his voice, opened his eyes. He gazed down at his hands. They were soft and somehow smaller. His robe was now red and then he realized that he and the stranger in the robe were now one—one heart, one body, one spirit.

Knarfi heard himself speaking, "Come sit, I have been expecting you. You should have been here yesterday." As he continued, the words flowed from Knarfi's mouth. "Enlightenment is a long and hard road. Why do you think you can rest on your journey?"

He now realized that there were three other men with him— he also realized that he himself was one of them, along with Naojo and Namder. Another chance was being given to his friends, and he was there both to participate in and to guide their adventure. He understood this as he now understood the oneness of the universe.

His friends would receive another chance, another chance to choose again. Would they choose from their heart this time? If not, he knew another opportunity would arise for them to choose again, and again, and again if necessary, until they chose the only real choice. All would eventually remember. All would ultimately choose love. Knarfi began to wonder in excitement and calmness what circumstance would arise to allow his friends to choose again, to choose from their heart, to choose enlightenment.

A Visit to Hospice

Years ago, when my first wife and I decided to end our marriage, I awoke one morning with a yearning somewhat like Knarfi, Naojo, and Namder's yearning to find enlightenment. My yearning, not as grandiose as finding enlightenment, was to do volunteer work.

"What type of volunteer work do you want to do?" my wife asked.

"I don't know, hospice work I suppose," I replied.

"Do you even know what a hospice is?"

I barely knew and later learned I was not the typical candidate. Most volunteers have either health care backgrounds or some past encounter with hospice. A mother, father, or grandparent died and hospice was a part of his or her transition. I had no healthcare background and no one close in my family had died. I was committing to do hospice volunteer work and I had no idea why!

That was many years ago. A year after I began volunteering, Lynn, another volunteer who works with me every Saturday morning, started volunteering. Driving into the city one morning, he had heard a radio advertisement for hospice. He drove directly to the hospice center and signed up to volunteer. He didn't have the typical background either, but somehow he knew it was something he was supposed to do.

Lynn and I have discussed how our hospice experience has changed our lives and we both agree that if you want to learn something about living, listen to the dying.

* * *

Over the years, I did listen and I heard a common story, a story that spoke to the heart, not the head. Corporate America does not teach listening to your heart in order to get ahead. Starting with my divorce, my life began to change in ways I could not imagine. Just like Knarfi's decision in our story to stay behind and take care of the great white bear on his search for enlightenment, wasting my time doing volunteer work seemed contrary to getting ahead. While his friends continued onward in their search for enlightenment, Knarfi took a chance and followed his heart. I was hearing a message to do the same. Could I follow my heart instead of my head as Knarfi had done?

Dr. Elisabeth Kübler-Ross, who defined the five stages of death and who spent a lifetime working with the dying, said:

> "The dying learn a great deal at the end of life, usually when it is too late to apply."[11]

I debated with myself. Were the dying wrong? Was I willing to risk my career on what they said was the most important thing in our lives? I had spent many years in my profession, working hard, slowly but surely climbing the corporate ladder. Could I risk it all based on the sentiments of the dying?

I decided to take a leap of faith and change how I approached my work and life. That giant leap led to surprising success in both my personal and professional life, just as Knarfi's decision to stay behind and care for the great white bear led to his surprising enlightenment. That leap of faith led me to an understanding of the entrainment factor. To understand how entrainment can change your life, the following chapters explore:

- the benefits of entrainment

- my story of how I became aware of entrainment

- the messages the dying were telling me

- and the most important lesson I learned from the dying.

The Benefits of Entrainment

The benefits of entrainment are enormous. I am amazed at how many techniques to improve and succeed have at their center the concept of entrainment. Peel away the layers, pry open the shell, look inside, and in most cases, we find a sparkling gem called entrainment. As you read this book, you will become aware of many ways in which entrainment can enrich your life. First, here are some specific measurable benefits from scientific studies in the areas of medicine, education, and business as compiled by the HeartMath Research Center.[12]

The Medical Benefits of Entrainment

Scientific studies prove that stress, the result of anger, worry, and anxiety, significantly increases our risk of heart disease and cardiac failure. Using stress levels to predict cancer and heart disease is six times more accurate than measuring cholesterol levels, or blood pressure, or examining a patient's history of smoking cigarettes. People unable to manage stress in their lives have a 40% higher death rate than people who manage and reduce stress.

Stress is the breeding ground for disease. It spawns conditions such as high blood pressure, elevated blood sugar levels, compromised immune functions, reduced cell repair and regeneration, brain cell destruction, chronic pain and fatigue, etc. Stress-related disorders account for between 70% and 90% of all appointments to primary care doctors. Estimates show employers pay more than $200 billion each year from stress-related issues such as absenteeism, burnout, medical insurance costs, worker's compensation, lower productivity, etc. These costs are more than the profits of all Fortune 500 companies combined.

How Entrainment Helps

Entrainment attacks stress and disease at two levels: physical and emotional. On the physical level, entrainment affects the production of hormones that regulate stress and the immune system.

Entrainment boosts our immune system to help us stay healthier. Entrainment causes an increase in the hormone immunoglobulin A (IgA), a vital ingredient in our immune system. After entrainment occurs, a person will experience a rise in IgA for up to 6 hours. In addition, entrainment can actually help us live longer, as an increase in the hormone dehydroepiandrosterone (DHEA), the anti-aging hormone, occurs during entrainment. The most significant health benefit might be the decrease in the production of the stress hormone cortisol. People learning entrainment benefit from lower blood pressure, improved heart rates, less hypertension, and overall greater vitality.

At the emotional level, participants who learned entrainment lowered stress by 22% and reduced depression by 34% during an eight-week study. Other emotional and mental advantages from entrainment include:

- Increased cognitive performance and learning

- Heightened intuition

- Increased creativity

- Greater confidence

- Better emotional stability

- Fewer negative feelings

- Increased happiness and feeling of peacefulness

- Decreased depression

- Fewer sleep disorders

The Educational Benefits of Entrainment

The major problems found in our academic institutions in the 1940s were students that chewed gum, made excessive noise, or were caught running in the halls. Today's students face drugs, guns, and sexual issues unimaginable to students of the 1940s. In addition, the pressure to excel academically has risen to new heights.

How Entrainment Helps

Students educated in entrainment techniques demonstrated not only better academic results, but also better skills in dealing with the emotional and social issues confronting this new generation of students. They felt better about themselves, were less likely to follow their peers blindly, and were more independent and confident in their abilities.

Practicing entrainment techniques led to increases in academic and classroom performances including:

- Increased understanding of academic materials
- Better test-taking performance
- Better work management skills
- Heightened energy and motivation
- Better focus on school work
- Improved communication skills
- More independent decision making

Students also demonstrated better emotional and social skills when applying entrainment techniques including:

- Increased stress management skills
- Better interpersonal skills
- Better relationships with teachers and peers
- Increased leadership behavior
- Reduction in harmful behavior, hostility and depression
- Less likelihood to succumb to peer pressure

The Business Benefits of Entrainment

Businesses spend between $10 and $20 billion dollars per year in stress-related hospital costs and absenteeism. Employees suffering from stress-related issues miss an average of 16 days per year compared to the national average of 4 to 6 days. While the medical benefits of entrainment address these business losses, it is in the areas of employee productivity and organizational efficiency that entrainment helps our businesses the most.

How Entrainment Helps

Studies show employing entrainment in business environments leads to:

- Increased creativity

- Better and more intuitive problem solving skills

- Better decision making skills

- Better communication

- Better team dynamics and meetings

- Increase in listening skills

- Significant increase in efficiency and focus

- Increase in clarity of goals

- Overall increase in happiness, contentment, and job satisfaction with overall decrease in the desire to leave the company

- Decrease in nervousness, tension, anxiety, burnout, and anger

* * *

The benefits of entrainment are far-reaching. They are applicable to almost every aspect of our lives: physical, mental, emotional, and spiritual. Understanding and applying the concepts of entrainment will help optimize and create more success in our lives; yet a successful life reflects something greater than the individual benefits of entrainment. A successful life reflects a way of thinking, acting, and seeing the world from a new perspective—a perspective that allows meaning and purpose to drive the enhanced successes that entrainment can produce.

My Story

Maybe it's a good thing, I thought, as I waved at the moving van that I had helped load pull out of the driveway. Loading the heavy pieces exhausted my body—in particular, the heavy items such as the dresser that had kept our clothes neatly folded and organized the way I had wanted my life and marriage to be: everything in its place so I knew where everything was, would be, and should be. Tucked away in the back of the top drawer—where so many of us keep a special piece of jewelry, or a picture, or in my mother's case the five coins blackened from the fire that took her first husband away—was a set of cloth swatches my wife had gotten me so I would know what color of clothes to buy. The professionals said I should wear the cool crisp colors associated with "winter", while she should wear the soft pastel blues, pinks, and yellows known as "summer" colors. Before my first wife and I met, my entire wardrobe consisted of pastels. I loved pastels, but according to the experts, they were not my colors. We ridded my closet of all pastels and replaced them with the cool crisp colors of "winter" that most complemented my hair and complexion.

Maybe not, I thought as the van turned the corner and disappeared. My life was inside that van. My wife (soon to be ex-wife) and my daughter were in the car that followed the van. We had stayed together an extra six months so our daughter could finish the school year before they moved to California, far away from the mountains of Colorado where I would stay. Packing the heavy items into the van had exhausted my body. The small items, however, had drained my soul. My daughter's bicycle brought back memories of spending hours walking beside her, holding on to the back of the seat until she was ready to ride the two-wheeled vehicle alone, without her father's help. Memories of her triumphantly gliding down the driveway seemed years away now as I stood watching her and the car she was in disappear. If only she would turn around and wave—she didn't. So I turned around and faced my house, my somewhat empty house, not our house, but my house. I couldn't find the courage to go inside. What was once a home with everything I valued was now only an empty shell. Nothing awaited me inside. I got in my car and started to drive. Our friends were her friends, not really mine, so I drove to the only place where I felt special, the hospice.

I remember when I interviewed to become a hospice volunteer. Asked if I had lost anyone special in my life, I replied that no one close to me had died recently. I didn't say that I knew the impending separation from my family would seem like a death to me.

Frances and Dot, two patients at the hospice, would help my spirits. It always lifted my spirits to talk with them, hold their hands, and let them know someone was there—that they were not alone. Now, I needed to know I wasn't alone.

I walked into room 428. The room was empty, no Frances, no books, no personal items, no hint that one week before I had sat by the bed holding her hand and telling her that everything would be OK, there was nothing to be afraid of. The empty feeling in my stomach felt emptier and sank farther towards my feet.

I walked the distance of the hall to room 435 to see Dot. It, too, was empty. I left the hospice without saying a word to anyone. The feeling in my stomach wouldn't go away anywhere in the near future, but my mind knew I would be OK. I wasn't dying. I was only going through a divorce.

Unlike Knarfi, who had the courage to follow his heart and stay behind while his friends continued their search for enlightenment, it would take several years of a growing fear of dying, with similar deathbed regrets that I routinely heard from dying hospice patients, before I would find the courage to alter how I was living my life. For a long time I believed, like many of us, that success required long hours and personal sacrifices. Being successful at work provided my family with the material items our society teaches us we all need. As the breadwinner, it was my role to provide the physical aspects of life, and I did it well—the hard work, the late nights, the travel, the sacrifices—all that effort got me was a failed marriage and a daughter who no longer looked up with admiration at her daddy. But hospice had gotten me through the difficult frontier of divorce, so I decided to take a chance and boldly step into a new stage of life, one I hoped would allow me not to die with the same regrets of which the dying often spoke.

* * *

Today, I no longer continually work the long hours the way I did then. Remarried, my current wife and I have a relationship of which most people only dream. My daughter and I have a wonderful relationship. I have great friends. I am happier in my profession than at any time in my career. I no longer feel I am sacrificing my life for work. Yet I believe I am more successful than ever, not only in my work but also in every aspect of my life. Sounds almost too good to be true, but it is true. I learned how to be successful in both life and work without sacrificing the things I value for that success.

How did it happen? It happened when I finally began to apply the lessons the patients at the hospice were teaching me as they looked back upon their lives while they prepared to die. I discarded the lessons and values I learned as an adult stepping through the doors of corporate America and applied the lessons the dying were telling me. These were the same lessons and values my parents had taught me as a child when life was simpler, easier, and more enjoyable. As a result, not only did my success in corporate America become easier, my enjoyment of life and work also returned!

I began to read about death and other related subjects. I already knew a lot about management theories. Corporate management theories preach something similar to what the dying preach, yet we rarely put these theories at the forefront of our corporate behavior. It sounds good, something we can tell our managers to practice, and something we can put down as goals on performance appraisals. Nevertheless, when the rubber meets the road, the corporate world is about getting things done, not those touchy-feely things spouted by the theorists.

My research into death and dying led me into studies about health, the human body, and eventually quantum physics. These provided hard evidence that there was a lot of truth and benefit in those touchy-feely concepts. I found new scientific discoveries supporting what the dying and the theorists say. Our sciences had uncovered not only evidence that entrainment worked, but also how it worked.

What Changed?

As I stepped into adulthood, I never thought to question why the rules we learned as children were not the rules by which we play as adults. I dutifully learned the new rules found in the real world of earning a living. The dying have a different view. They say the right rules are actually the ones we learned as children. I found that using the rules and strategies taught to us by our parents produced the same effects as the rules of corporate America and adulthood, but with a fraction of the effort. Generations of parents have taught their children these principles, and generations of children have abandoned them as they moved into the harsh world of adulthood. Yet they teach their children the same principles because somewhere inside they know, or hope, there is truth within these principles. Our fear of the unknown perils of adulthood snatches away these principles, replacing them with new principles based on the cold, hard, cruel world. A new truth, firmly rooted in the world as seen from the eyes of adults, replaces the simple principles of childhood. Our childhood beliefs offer little resistance to the powerful and established truth of the marching army called adulthood and the real world.

In the adult world, the search for truth follows a path of twists, turns, and surprises that often resists the truth when it presents itself. We hold tightly to the old truth, resisting the new with hope it is wrong. At one time, our earth was flat. At one time, our earth was the center of the universe. In 1543, Nicolaus Copernicus published *De revolutionibus* and proposed the earth revolved around the sun. Eighty-nine years later, with proof to support him, Galileo Galilei published his *Dialogue Concerning the Two Chief World Systems, Ptolematic and Copernican*, stating in his preface that the arguments within in no way supported the Copernican view of the heavens, but were presented to show that the Holy Church understood both views. The following year, in 1633, he stood trial for heresy. Galileo's reward for placing the truth on our doorstep was house arrest for the remainder of his life. In 1687, Sir Isaac Newton published his *Principia* to explain the laws of motion and gravitation, yet it was another 135 years before the Holy Church permitted publications that taught the motion of the planets. Not until 1835, some 202 years after Galileo published his *Dialogue*, was the book removed from the Holy Church's Index of Prohibited Books.[13]

Copernicus's discovery that the earth travels around the sun awoke a multitude of inquiring minds that would not rest until the world accepted the truth about the earth's relationship to the heavens. Copernicus's discovery started a scientific movement to unfold the mystery of the universe. However, quantum physicists looked into the microscope only to discover the *mysteries* of our ancestors' philosophies and concepts glaring back at them. The physicist Fritjof Capra indicates that the new discoveries in the world of quantum physics suggest a world very much like that described by Eastern mysticism.[14]

Newtonian physics easily explains the world in which we live. An apple falls from a tree, strikes Sir Isaac Newton on the head, and modern Newtonian physics is born. Newtonian physics explains such things as the velocity of the apple, its acceleration, and the gravitational force applied to the apple. Quantum physics and our ancestors' philosophies somehow find themselves explaining the relationship among the apple, Sir Isaac, and his resulting theory of physics. At the quantum level, they somehow are all interconnected.

As quantum physics uncovers the truths and secrets of the universe, showing us there is more than the physics of Sir Isaac Newton, reexamining the teaching and concepts we learned as children reveal there is more than the practices of the western world, corporate America, and adulthood. Applying the simple teaching of children to our modern way of living can show us a truer way to approach both work and play.

Most of the concepts are not new. They are the concepts we learned as children and put aside as we grew into adults. Renewing the practice of these concepts is not difficult as long as we let go of some of our adult attachments.

Sometimes it takes children to show us the true meaning of the concepts we try to teach them. Gregg Braden, in his book *The Isaiah Effect*, tells a story about nine physically and/or mentally challenged children participating in the 1998 Special Olympics who became friends. During one of the races, one of the contestants fell at the start of the race. One boy with Down's Syndrome noticed his fallen friend and quite naturally turned around, walked back to his friend, and helped him up. Gradually, every contestant in the race noticed, and one by one, they all walked back to their friend, and they all locked arms and walked to cross the finish line simultaneously. To this group of special children, friendship had beaten the glory of winning.[15]

Letting go of some of our adult attachments to how we can have a successful life allows us to begin to practice the entrainment factor, where we begin to experience Carl Jung's concept of *synchronicity*. We begin to notice change taking place on the inside and manifesting itself on the outside. We begin to notice that the minute, the quantum pieces too small to make a difference, defines the difference between success and failure.

What The Dying Were Telling Me

Sara was supposed to die quickly when she came to hospice. The cancer had spread rapidly, but she did not die. Three months slipped by before she told me that she had not spoken with her brother in twenty years. She was not sure about what they had even argued. I urged her to call her brother, finally convincing her with the question "If he were dying, would you want to know?" Somehow, she found the courage as she faced the end of her life to do something she could not do when she had good health and mental strength—she reached out and called her brother. Death has a way of making even the living do things they would not normally do, so her brother came to visit Sara. They spent one week together. Her brother left on a Sunday. Sara died two days later on a Tuesday.

Sara's lesson was simple: she had matters of the heart to take care of before she died, before her life's work would be complete, before she could declare success and go home for the day.

* * *

Donald had been a chief scientist at one of our largest American corporations. Numerous times, he had stood before our Senate and Congress giving technology briefings in his area of expertise. Donald told me he wanted to figure it out before he died—figure out what life was about. I visited with Donald every Saturday for almost four months.

"What have you learned, Donald?" I asked him.

"Caring, Gabriel, there is so much caring here. I never noticed it before. My family, my children, my grandchildren—they have demonstrated so much caring I never noticed before."

Donald did not die the way most people die in a hospice. Most people's body fails them slowly. Taken away are the freedoms we take for granted each day: walking, feeding ourselves, taking a shower, and going to the bathroom alone. Donald was fine on Thursday morning. On Thursday night, he died in his sleep of a heart attack.

* * *

The message of the dying is simple: love is the most important thing we do in our lifetime. This contradicts conventional thinking about what leads to greater success in our professional careers. I wanted to be successful, and part of that was having people I loved in my life, but love was only one aspect of my definition of success. The dying, however, say it is the only real aspect.

One man, a man whom I had never met, pushed me over the edge and gave me the courage to try an experiment at work. In order to be hypnotized, you have to focus on the spoken voice or a swinging watch, but you have to focus on the right thing or it does not work. Dannion Brinkley learned to focus the hard way.

One day, as he talked on the telephone, lightning descended to the ground and through the telephone wires. In an instant too small for us to grasp, Dannion Brinkley was grasped by lightning. The nails in his shoes were welded to the nails of the floor on which he stood, his body was thrown across the room from the many volts of electricity that entered it, and the telephone lay melted in his hand. One moment, Dannion spoke to a friend over the phone; the next moment his body lay lifeless on the other side of the room. As the ambulance carrying Dannion's body sped towards the hospital, the medic inside informed Dannion's wife that they were too late; Dannion was dead.

At the hospital, they made heroic efforts to revitalize Dannion, but eventually they wheeled him into the hall for transport to the morgue. His friend, the other party on the telephone line when lightning took Dannion's life away, stood next to the gurney, watching the white sheet that covered the still, lifeless body. Twenty-eight minutes had passed since the medic in the ambulance indicated Dannion was dead. Twenty-eight minutes would pass between one breath and, by some miracle, another one. Somehow, Dannion had returned. He was alive. He could not move, so he did the only thing he could—he breathed a new breath, a new life. His friend noticed the sheet as it began ever so slowly to move up and down above Dannion's mouth. "He's alive!" he shouted.[16]

My friends at hospice, who face death, tell me a simple message about the importance of caring. Dannion delivered the same message from the insight he gained from being dead for twenty-eight minutes. Dannion brought the message that we are here to create good, and that you get to experience and feel all the good things you do in your life when you die. He indicates that it is not big bold actions that create the good; rather, it is the individual acts, the little acts of kindheartedness that reflect who we really are that count.[17]

* * *

Dr. Elisabeth Kübler-Ross and her colleague interviewed over twenty thousand people who had died and, by some form of medical intervention or miracle, returned from the official state known as death. Twenty thousand people told similar stories of leaving their bodies, traveling through a tunnel of light, and meeting a being of pure love. Many got as far as a life review, but all were sent back or were given the choice to return. Twenty thousand people gave the same reason as to why we are here—the same reason Donald and so many others at the hospice have told me as they face death— the reason according to the twenty thousand people interviewed by Dr Kübler-Ross: love.[18]

Our Life Purpose

Sara, Donald, Dot, Frances, and many other hospice patients left this world with one piece of advice for me: life is not about our careers; it's about our relationships with our family, our friends, our co-workers, and anyone else that enters our lives. When they were absorbed in their careers, many felt that it was the most important aspect of their life. Why else would we be willing to sacrifice so much for our careers: our private lives, our time with our family and friends, sometimes our health? When the dying looked back and reviewed their lives, their most common regret was too much effort spent on their careers and not enough effort on their relationships with family, friends, and co-workers.

As a man in his late forties, I began to wonder whether I would utter the same words of wisdom to those around me when I lie on my deathbed. Would I look back on my life and conclude that our relationships with our families, our friends, our neighbors, and our co-workers compose the real importance of our lives? Would I have regrets for not listening to the words of wisdom that the dying whispered to me? Could I ignore the twenty thousand who spoke similar words to Dr. Elisabeth Kübler-Ross and her colleague? Twenty thousand people who experienced a near-death experience say our life purpose is to learn about and practice love. How can one ignore such wisdom? If we listen to the dying, they repeat a simple message about living: the reason we are here is love. Our life purpose according to the dying:

We are here to learn about and practice love.

Our success ABCs assert that our *attitude* determines the *behavior* that causes the *consequences*. The dying reveal that the right attitude is simple:

Attitudes of love, caring, and compassion determine the behavior that causes the consequences that lead to a successful life.

While fear and regret are powerful motivators, it was caring that eventually convinced me to change my life to avoid at my death the regrets I so often heard. I cared about my life. Somehow fulfilling my life purpose seemed more important than the petty trials and tribulations I faced each day at work. Understanding that there is a purpose for my life—that we are here to learn about and practice love—gave new meaning to why I am here and what is important. For me, having a life purpose brought clarity to my life.

John Grey, the author of *Men are From Mars, Women are from Venus*, decided to place his love for his wife above his career. What happened? He became more successful in his career. I, too, finally decided to place my life purpose above my career, and to my surprise, my career became more successful.

Principle 1: Purpose

Purpose is the first of five principles in understanding how to live a successful life. Having a purpose is not entrainment, but understanding that our life purpose is to learn about and practice love is a critical element in the entrainment factor. How important to success is having a purpose? Recent studies on what makes companies great reveal that great companies need to have a purpose. Jim Collins, author of two national bestsellers, *Built to Last: Successful Habits of Visionary Companies* and *Good to Great: Why Some Companies Make the Leap...and Others Don't*, states that purpose is what gives meaning to our work.[19]

Examine the core purpose of some of the visionary and great corporations as presented in *Built to Last*:

Examples of Core Purpose:

*"**3M**: To solve unsolved problems innovatively"*

*"**Cargill**: To improve the standard of living around the world"*

*"**Fannie Mae**: To strengthen the social fabric by continually democratizing home ownership"*

*"**Hewlett-Packard**: To make technical contributions for the advancement and welfare of humanity"*

*"**Mary Kay**: To give unlimited opportunity to women"*

*"**McKinsey**: To help leading corporations and governments to be more successful"*

*"**Merck**: To preserve and improve human life"*

*"**Sony**: Experience the joy of advancing and applying technology for the benefit of the public"*

*"**Wal-Mart**: To give ordinary folk the chance to buy the same things as rich people"*

*"**Walt Disney**: To make people happy"*[20]

Purpose is the reason we do something. William Hewlett and David Packard had a passion for technology. They formed Hewlett-Packard as a company to be able to express their passion; but behind their passion and skills, they each had a desire to help make the world a better place to live, as reflected in their company purpose:

*"**Hewlett-Packard**: To make technical contributions for the advancement and welfare of humanity"*[21]

Mary Kay Ash wanted to help women excel in business. To give women opportunity, she created a company that inherently took advantage of the interest almost every adolescent girl pursues—cosmetics. Creating a company centered on cosmetics became the strategy Mary Kay Ash used to fulfill her purpose.

*"**Mary Kay**: To give unlimited opportunity to women"*[22]

Walt Disney had an innate desire to make children happy. Walt used his skills, creativity, and interests to create cartoons and theme parks as a strategy to fulfill his purpose.

*"**Walt Disney**: To make people happy"*[23]

Our strategy, *how we do something*, is different from our purpose. Our purpose is *why* we do something, the reason that motivates us to reach out, take risks, find answers, and make things happen. Understanding what motivates us becomes a powerful tool in creating success. It is powerful because our purpose gives meaning to our lives while also acting as a beacon of light to guide and illuminate our paths. Jim Collins, in his best-selling business book *Built to Last*, emphasizes the importance for companies to have a purpose. Collins' research shows that a company's purpose acts both as a source for inspiration and as an overall guiding light in which to make decisions.[24]

Our purpose acts as our guide, leading us when we become lost, disoriented or overwhelmed by our surroundings. Few of us would go on a safari without hiring a local guide to show us our way and protect us from danger. Re-examine the purposes of the companies listed above: they are not companies whose purpose is to make money. In *Built to Last*, Collins indicates that a company's reason for existence, its purpose, is what defines the organization's soul. Collins references a speech from David Packard (co-founder of Hewlett-Packard) in which Packard emphasizes that a company must find a deeper reason for existing than simply to make money. [25]

David H. Maister, an expert on the management of professional companies, states in his book *Practice What you Preach—What Managers Must Do to Create a High Achievement Culture* that "chasing money is not what makes you money."[26] Numerous other studies confirm Collins and Maister's findings about what David Packard expressed—successful companies are guided by their purpose for existence; money results from achieving that purpose.

Similarly, a successful life comes not from a focus on acquiring wealth and happiness. Rather, achieving wealth and happiness comes from finding and fulfilling our purpose. At the highest level, our life purpose—to learn about and practice love—should serve as a guiding light by which we live our lives. Almost every core purpose for the companies listed above reflects our life purpose in one form or another:

- *"To solve unsolved problems innovatively"*
- *"To improve the standard of living around the world"*
- *"To strengthen the social fabric by continually democratizing home ownership"*
- *"To make technical contributions for the advancement and welfare of humanity"*
- *"To give unlimited opportunity to women"*
- *"To help leading corporations and governments to be more successful"*
- *"To preserve and improve human life"*
- *"Experience the joy of advancing and applying technology for the benefit of the public"*

- *"To give ordinary folk the chance to buy the same things as rich people"*

- *"To make people happy"*[27]

We feel better when trying to make the world better rather than working for a company whose only goal is to make money.

* * *

Our life purpose—to learn and practice love—is not as obvious to us as it sounds. We see hints and glimpses of it throughout our lives. Some people are fortunate enough to understand our life purpose while others are not. Regardless, we all pursue our life purpose whether we are consciously aware of it or not. Our basic drives to find mates, raise families and enjoy friends provide a natural learning arena to discover and practice the concept of love.

Becoming aware of our individual and career purposes, which should be subsets of our life purpose, is often a process of self-discovery. Sometimes our individual and career purposes are clear and present in our lives. A more common scenario is that we are not fully aware of what our individual and career purposes are, but we do catch glimpses and insight into what they might be throughout our lives. In my case, I did not clearly understand my career purpose until quite some time after I began working with hospice patients, which eventually led me to understand my life purpose. Examine my career purpose before and after I understood my life purpose:

Career Purpose Before: Climb the corporate ladder to advance my position and salary in order to be a good provider for my family.

Career Purpose After: Help others be successful.

While my "before' career purpose had a noble objective (be a good provider for my family), it provided no guidance as to how I could accomplish that objective. How would I climb the corporate ladder? In addition, I made the cardinal sin of establishing making money as my purpose. Making money should be the by-product, not the objective.

My "after" career purpose establishes a clear and specific guideline to follow: help others be successful. This is a very specific guideline. How I go about accomplishing that purpose is strategy, which we will examine in the next section of this book. Whether I am working as a corporate executive or giving lectures, seminars, and workshops on entrainment, my purpose is clear: help others be successful. My career purpose serves as a guiding light by which I can make decisions. If I am making career decisions that go against my guiding light, then I need to rethink my decision. The entrainment factor can help. Using entrainment, as we will discover, can help expand perspectives so that a new solution arises.

* * *

Whereas our career purpose establishes guidelines for our professional life, our individual purpose creates guidelines for our personal life. As we bring our personal and professional lives into alignment with our life purpose, we often find our personal and career purposes merging. Using our life purpose as our guiding principle ensures that our personal and career purposes complement one another, and do not create opposing forces in our lives.

A personal purpose relates to our personal life: what we find important outside of our professional careers. My personal purpose revolves around my family, primarily by providing for them. Family is often a central theme in personal purposes, and there are many variations on that theme. My wife, a professional educator for over 30 years, finds her personal purpose centered on rearing children. This closely aligns with her career purpose and finds its expression in teaching third grade.

Applying the Principle of Purpose

Having a life, career or personal purpose provides a sense of calmness akin to that found in the center of a tornado. Everything else may be in chaos, but somehow that purpose provides a sense of peace, understanding and guidance, allowing you to put one foot in front of the other and move forward.

Having a light when walking in a cave seems like basic common sense; but what if you don't have a light? What happens if you don't yet know your life, career, or personal purpose? Fortunately, you can apply the concept of purpose to almost anything you do.

At its basic level, purpose is understanding what or why you are doing something. Not understanding *what* is the cause of more failures than can be imagined. In my field, software development, 86% of software projects fail to meet functionality, cost, or schedule with the number one reason for failure being a lack of requirements management—that is, not managing the *what*. Consider the following true story.

Scotty, a project manager, stopped by the cubicle of his friend Eric, who told him about an exciting staffing tool his manager had assigned him to build. Scotty saw Eric's enthusiasm as he explained how the tool would work, but something didn't seem right. Being a manager himself, Scotty could not understand how the tool would actually benefit Eric's manager. Scotty encouraged his friend to meet with his manager and get a fuller understanding of the tool before proceeding.

Six weeks later, Scotty again stopped by Eric's cube. Eric, bursting with pride, told Scotty he was putting the final changes on the tool and would show it to his manager the next day. Scotty asked if Eric had taken his advice and reviewed what he was building with his manager. Eric had not, but was sure his manager would love the tool.

The following day Eric stopped by Scotty's office, informing him that his manager was having him rewrite the tool—it was not what his manager had expected. It took another four weeks to finish the project.

Eric spent ten weeks to complete a six-week project for the simple reason that he did not have a clear understanding of *what* he was actually building. Unfortunately, this is a common story. Simply making sure that Eric clearly understood the "purpose" of the tool would have saved four weeks of work.

Outwardly, Eric's lack of clearly understanding *what* he needed to do cost the company four weeks of work. Inwardly, there were additional and potentially longer-term damages. First, consider Eric's embarrassment, frustration and disappointment at not meeting his manager's expectations: in missing the original schedule, in his ability to work independently and in his ability to do the work. Next, consider the negative image created in his manager's mind—an image that may take numerous projects for Eric to overcome.

The outward damage of four weeks of lost work is of less importance than the potential inward damages to Eric's career.

*　*　*

Tom and Mary celebrated their two-year anniversary of being together. Mary recalled how they had met and how she had fallen in love with Tom. She loved Tom dearly and found herself asking Tom what he wanted in a relationship. He wanted to have fun and just be together. When Tom asked Mary what she wanted, she said she hadn't given it much thought, but what she really wanted was to settle down and eventually have a family. She wanted to know when she came home that someone would be there to eat dinner with her, help with the kids, and hold her at night when they went to bed. Tom admitted he could never see himself as a father, at least not for many years to come. Both Mary and Tom made a discovery about their relationship that night—what they each wanted in a relationship was different and not compatible. It wasn't long before they went their separate ways, each seeking a new path that they hoped would bring them a relationship providing what they wanted. Only when Tom and Mary took a good look at *what* they wanted, and *what* they were doing in their relationship, were they able to realize that they each were walking a path not leading to where they wanted to go. Without examining the *what* of their relationship, they could have spent several more years until they realized that they would never be satisfied together.

*　*　*

These are just two examples of how clearly understanding *what* you are doing can help you achieve your goals in a more efficient and effective way. In Eric's case, clearly knowing *what* he was building would have resulted in working less and accomplishing more. In Tom and Mary's case, their relationship had matured to the point where they needed to take a good look at *what* they wanted and *what* they were doing together. In doing so, they were able to avoid doing more (staying in their relationship) and accomplishing less (not getting what they wanted).

Get in the habit of making sure you clearly understand *what* you are trying to accomplish. It should be the first step in any project you undertake. It brings clarity to your actions. It acts as a guiding light, ensuring that you are going in the right direction. It allows you to be effective with your time. It is the first step in doing less and accomplishing more.

* * *

Principle Summary

<u>**Successful Living ABCs:**</u> Our *attitude* determines the *behavior* that causes the *consequences*.

> ***Attitudes*** *of love, caring, and compassion result in the* ***Behavior*** *that causes the* ***Consequences*** *that lead to a successful life.*

LIFE PRINCIPLES :

> <u>**Purpose:**</u> To learn about and practice love.

* * *

A purpose is not something you make up; rather, it is something you discover, nurture, and allow to spring forth to become a clear and guiding light in your life. The following worksheets provide an opportunity to examine your own purpose, whether it is a personal or career purpose. Attempt to write down your purpose. Set it aside and try it again once you have finished this book, but don't stop there. Periodically, examine what you have written and rewrite your purpose until you feel it expresses and captures what is truly important to you. Remember, a purpose expresses what is important to you, what motivates you, why you do the things you do. A purpose is not strategy; it doesn't describe how you "make people happy" or "create unlimited opportunity for women" or "help others be successful." It also doesn't have to be something grandiose or glamorous. A male nurse at the hospice where I volunteer loves people. He likes to interact frequently with people and help them. He knows that this is who he is. It is his purpose. He may not be able to express it, but from the outside looking in, it is obvious. He could have chosen many ways to follow his purpose; he chose to be a nurse. It allows him to be with people and to help people. It allows him to fulfill his purpose. From a spiritual perspective, by fulfilling his purpose and expressing it through being a nurse, at the end of his life he will review and judge it as a successful one.

* * *

To help you begin the process of discovering and understanding your purpose, Worksheet A asks you to review your life. What is important to you? What trends and patterns have occurred in your life, and do they provide insight into who you are and what your purpose may be? Answer the questions on the worksheet. Spend time reflecting about your life, what you value, and why you value those things.

For instance, Joan, a victim of an abusive childhood, began working with abused children and eventually opened her own center after she realized that her life experience had prepared her for this work and given her special insight into what it means to live as an abused child. She discovered that her purpose and passion was to help others who are victims of a childhood similar to hers.

Worksheet B asks you to try to express your purpose in words. Don't be frustrated if you have trouble or cannot identify or express your purpose. Understanding your purpose can take time. This book provides additional information, allowing you to access untapped potential to help bring your purpose to the surface.

If you are not ready to identify your personal or professional purpose, use Worksheet B to practice applying the principle of purpose to a project, task, or activity you are undertaking to see if it changes or clarify your approach.

For example, a general manager directed a team to implement a set of industry-standard software development practices. From the very start, the team encountered resistance from the organization's first-line managers. Realizing that they were not making acceptable progress, they revisited their assignment with the general manager, where they learned the real goal behind the assignment was to make the organization better. Implementing a set of development standards was not the real goal, but rather it was the general manager's solution as to how to make the organization better; it was the *how,* not the *what.*

With a new understanding of *what* they were doing, they expanded their thinking and changed their approach with the first-line managers. Instead of forcing standards upon the organization, the team looked at ways to improve the organization and implement standards where and when the time was right. This changed the first-line manager's attitude about the team from "those people trying to tell us how to do our jobs" to "those people who are willing to help us".

The general manager had given the team a solution—the *how*—without allowing the team to fully understand the problem—the *what*. Clearly understanding *what* the general manager really wanted cleared the path for the team to be more creative and allowed for more progress.

* * *

Understanding our life purpose is the first step in living a successful life. Dannion Brinkley's near-death experience and life-review reveals that it is not through bold actions that our life's purpose is accomplished; rather, it is through small, repeated acts of kindness that we accomplish our life objective.

Knowing our life purpose is the first step in living a successful life. It may take some time for you to identify your professional or personal purpose, but don't worry. Start applying the principle of purpose: clearly understanding *what* you are trying to accomplish for any task, action, or project you undertake. It is the first step in doing less and accomplishing more.

Principle 1 – Purpose

Worksheet A

Identify Your Purpose: Use the following questions to help you understand and discover your purpose.

What is important to you? Describe what is important in your personal or professional life and why each item is important. Are the reasons they are important acceptable to you?

_____
_____
_____
_____
_____

Who are you? Write a brief paragraph describing yourself.

_____
_____
_____
_____
_____
_____
_____
_____

Life Trends: Reflect back on your life to identify any trends, pattern, or significant events that have occurred. What lessons do you believe these trends are trying to teach you? Do they provide any insight into who you are and what your purpose may be?

_____

_____

_____

_____

_____

_____

_____

_____

_____

Principle 1 – Purpose

Worksheet B

Identifying the WHAT: Write your personal or career purpose and / or select a task, activity or project you have underway or plan to start. Clearly state *what* you are trying to accomplish.

Purpose: Describe your personal or career purpose.

_____

_____

_____

_____

_____

What: Select a project or activity and clearly describe what problem is being solved.

_____

_____

_____

_____

_____

Section 2 - Strategy

"A Dull Blade Does Not Cut"

Unknown

Our joyful living ABCs teach that our *attitude* determines the *behavior* that causes the *consequences*.

Attitude leads to **B**ehavior which leads to **C**onsequences which equals **Success & Happiness**

A + B + C = Success and Happiness

The dying say that caring is the secret to life. If we listen to them, we can deduce that *attitudes of love, caring and compassion* determine the *behavior* that causes the *consequences* that lead to a successful life. However, what do our scientists say? This section examines the hard science of entrainment and the conclusions about the right attitude needed to create a successful life.

From what we discover in recent scientific findings, we arrive at our second life principle: strategy.

Strategy: A Story

"Grandfather, see the bird on the roof? It's very beautiful, isn't it," a young boy said as he pointed to the roof of the old man's hut.

"Yes, it is very beautiful indeed," came the reply from the old man. "Sit and I shall tell you a story about a beautiful bird. Actually, it is about two beautiful birds. I will tell you about visitors and an adventure that happened right here in this village—and it happened to me," the old man said. And with these words he captured the attention of the little boy who now sat in front of him.

"Many years ago, there were two visitors from a faraway land," the old man began.

"Where did they come from?" asked the little boy.

"From America," came the reply.

"Someday, I will go to America," the boy said.

"I have been to America," the grandfather said.

"You have been to America?" the little boy asked with excitement.

"Yes, I have, and if you do not interrupt, I will tell you the complete story," the grandfather replied. "Now, many years ago there were two visitors who traveled from America in search of a guru. They were led to this very village and to this very house—my house."

"Why to your house, grandfather?" the boy asked.

"Well, they came to find something, and they believed that I was the one who could help them find it. But they were mistaken. As they left, I gave each one of them a beautiful bird, as beautiful as the one you saw sitting on top of the roof a little while ago. I told them perhaps the bird could help them find what they were looking for."

"How could a bird find something?" the boy asked.

"Sometimes, answers come in many ways," the grandfather answered. "Many years later, I received a letter from one of the visitors asking me to come to America to visit. They would pay for all my expenses."

"So you went to America?" the boy asked.

"Yes, I did, but not without asking to also see the other visitor. This took some effort as the two had parted shortly after returning from visiting this village. Finally it was arranged, and I flew on the big silver bird across the ocean to America.

"Now, upon arriving at the first visitor's house, I found that he was very excited to see me. We shared tea and conversation for many hours. He lived alone, except for his pet bird— the very bird I had given him. After spending the day together, he wanted me to see his bird. We walked from his garden to the main living area of his house. As we walked, he spoke of how he loved his bird. I could tell that the bird provided great comfort to him. He told me that he shared his problems with his pet bird. Although people would not listen, he said that the bird always listened to his problems.

"Entering the room, I saw the beautiful bird in a large golden cage. It was wonderful. He began to speak with the bird. I could tell he depended greatly on his bird. Yes, he truly loved this bird. It provided him with companionship and friendship. While other people in his life would come and go, he could always depend on his bird to listen to his problems. I could sense the bird gave him the strength to keep going each day.

"I asked if I might hold the bird. He refused my request for fear the bird, if let outside its cage, would fly away. At that point he confessed it was the bird that helped him find the answers for which he had been searching when he visited our village. I left him knowing that the bird gave him great comfort and that my friend felt gratitude to and great love for the bird in the beautiful golden cage."

"So the bird taught him about love?" the little boy asked the grandfather.

"Very good, it would seem that way wouldn't it?" the grandfather said.

"Now, several days later, I found myself at the home of the second visitor," the grandfather continued. "Again, I spent most of the day talking and visiting with this second visitor to our village. Near the end of the day, she wished to show me her treasure. We went into her back yard. It was a magnificent yard, full of trees, shrubs, and beautiful flowers. I relayed it was indeed a very beautiful treasure. She agreed it was a beautiful yard. However, she wanted to show me a different treasure. She instructed me to be still and remain quiet. It was peaceful there as the sounds of nature provided tranquility.

"Then, quite suddenly, something rushed past my head from behind. It happened too quickly for me to be startled, and I stood amazed as I stared at a small yellow bird that had landed on my friend's shoulder."

"Was it the bird?" asked the boy.

"Yes, exactly," the grandfather said. "Then, she held up her hand with one finger pointing outward. The bird hopped onto the outstretched finger and she proceeded to tell me about the bird. The bird provided comfort and companionship to her, just as the other visitor's bird did for him. Soon, however, I saw a squirrel climb down a tree. Other animals became visible. I wondered if they had been there the whole time. There were butterflies, a hummingbird, and two cats playing.

"We talked awhile, and eventually she told the bird that supper was ready and gently tossed the bird into the air. The bird flew away, circled, and flew directly into an open window on the second floor of her home.

"Curious, I asked her a question, and she took me back into the house and to the room on the second floor. There, inside another beautiful birdcage, sat the bird. She asked if I would like to hold the bird. She instructed me to reach into the cage and place my finger beside the bird. The bird jumped onto my finger, and I removed my hand and the bird from the cage.

"After some time, the bird flew out the open window. She told me that the first time she had allowed the bird its freedom, she wondered whether she would ever see the bird again. In spite of the comfort and joy the bird provided, she couldn't bear to see the bird locked in the cage. She had imagined what it would be like if *she* were trapped in a cage.

"It was her love for the bird that made her realize that it must be free to choose its own way. She said that a bird in a cage is not a pet bird—it is simply a caged bird. A pet bird is one who is there by choice, not because it is locked behind a closed cage door."

"So she too learned about love from the bird!" the little boy said.

"Yes, she too learned about love," the grandfather assured the young boy. "But the story is more than a story of love. The story is also about fear."

"But I wasn't scared," the little boy interjected.

"No, not that kind of fear," the grandfather said as he reached over and hugged the small child. Placing the boy in his lap, he continued. "It is about the fear of *losing* love. Sometimes we believe we must hold on tight or we will lose those things we value and treasure, when in actuality, the world works in quite the opposite way! If you want something, then give it away," the grandfather said. "You will be surprised how quickly and abundantly the universe will return it."

"I want to be happy," the boy responded.

"Then go and put a smile on someone's face," the grandfather said.

The little boy jumped down from his grandfather's lap and ran off. The grandfather smiled.

The Key to a Successful Life

This section presents the concept of *entrainment*—the key behind creating a successful life. The benefits of entrainment are significant, yet dwarfed when compared to the simplicity of how we can create entrainment in our lives. Through simple techniques, common sense habits, and an awareness of how entrainment works, everyone can enjoy the benefits, advantages, and dramatic shift towards a successful life that entrainment brings. In this section, we explore:

- what entrainment is,

- how it works, and

- how we can learn to employ it to bring success to our personal and professional lives.

The concept of entrainment is not new. The scientific term has been around since 1666, when Christiann Huygens invented the pendulum clock. Whenever he placed a new clock in his shop, he noticed a strange phenomenon: the clock's pendulum would soon begin to swing in unison with the other clocks. In fact, all of the clocks' pendulums would swing in unison with each other. Whenever he reset them to swing on different rhythms, they soon synchronized themselves and swung in unison again. Scientists later would determine that the largest pendulum would pull the others into its rhythm, resulting in a unified beat among all the pendulums. This phenomenon is *entrainment* and it appears frequently throughout nature.[28]

An obvious example appears in the menstrual cycles of women who live together. Often their cycles synchronize, *entrained* according to the terminology of the 17th century. Another type of entrainment—between the heart and the brain—provides the advantages that can transform our personal and professional lives. When the brain and the heart enter into a state of entrainment (i.e., when the alpha brain waves and heart rhythms are synchronized), we experience an "intelligent flow of awareness and insight."[29] At a very high level, heart / brain entrainment creates a state in which individuals experience heightened creativity, problem solving, decision-making, and intuition.

Experiments at companies such as Sears, Motorola and MCI demonstrate the advantages of teaching techniques to induce heart / brain entrainment in employees. The companies realized measurable increases in productivity, teamwork, health and a definite improvement in the corporate bottom line.[30] Subjects who learned how to induce heart / brain entrainment reported "increased mental clarity and intuition" while reducing stress and increasing effectiveness, and "their perception of problems or difficult situations often widened enough that new perspectives and solutions emerged."[31]

Experiencing the benefits and tremendous advantages gained by employing entrainment in our daily lives, we greatly increase our odds of being successful. The secret to utilizing entrainment lies in understanding how entrainment works. To understand how entrainment works we must:

- shatter some myths about how one finds success and happiness,

- examine the recent scientific discoveries in the field of medicine that reveal the power behind entrainment, and

- explore how we activate that power.

This section dives into the science behind how our brain and emotions work to create heart / brain entrainment. I have tried to keep these scientific discussions brief and as non-scientific as possible. A scientific understanding of heart / brain entrainment allows us to realize how we can easily activate heart / brain entrainment to bring success and happiness into our lives.

The Myth of Logic

There was a time in our history when thinking or suggesting that the Earth was not flat or that the Earth was not the center of the Universe was blasphemous. It took brave individuals like Columbus, Magellan, Copernicus and Galileo to prove that the accepted truth was not the actual truth.

In the business world and many aspects of our lives, the Western perspective holds tightly onto the concepts of logic and hard science. Consider a study of 250 executives that showed they did not believe the heart could, or should, be used in making business decisions. They believed that compassion and empathy would interfere in making the hard decisions required in the business world.[32]

At one time, I agreed with the 250 executives who said the heart has no place in the business world—our heads, not our hearts, determine our success. However, key heterogeneous discoveries from a group of brave new doctors, physicists, psychologists, sociologists and neurosurgeons are revealing a non-traditional solution on how we can create success in our lives. They are telling a story very similar to the stories I heard from my dying hospice patients. They are telling a story about the importance of caring, compassion and love in our quest for success and happiness.

* * *

Hospice is not the first place where I heard the opinion that love and compassion are critical elements in our quest for success. As a corporate executive and manager, I know motivated employees are critical to the success of a company, yet typical everyday corporate behavior contradicts known motivational theory. Theories and practices such as the Motivation / Hygiene theory, Theory Y, Theory Z, Participative Management, Team Building, Flattened Organizational Structures, Quality Circles, Fish Tales, etc., are among our modern motivational techniques. An amazing common factor in all of the above principles is something called the "Hawthorne Effect." The Hawthorne Effect resulted from a study done by Elton Mayo in the late 1920s and early 1930s at the Western Electric Hawthorne plant. Mayo conducted studies to determine what working conditions (such as duration of breaks, lighting, temperature, etc.) affected productivity. Many believe he uncovered the fundamental concept on which our various modern theories of motivation are based. In essence, the Hawthorne Effect says:

> Increased productivity happens when workers experience the *feeling of being cared about*—by the attitudes and actions of their managers and from being part of a team.

Yet our 250 executives indicated that they believed they needed to be emotionally aloof. In the workplace, their jobs demanded logic, not feelings. Allowing compassion and empathy in their style would never work.[33] I sat in executive meetings in which executives and managers discussed how to instill the sense of "being cared about" in their employees. The idea to start caring about the employees never arose.

While executives wanted to make employees *feel* cared about, they did not actually want to *care* about the employees; their only goal was increased productivity and motivation. As long as they could trick the employees into feeling cared about, they felt that their job was complete. The idea to start actually caring about their employees was a foreign concept in this group of brilliant high achievers.

The dying say that love is central to a successful life, and the Hawthorne Effect says caring makes the difference in our productivity at work. How do we find the courage and determination, as Columbus, Magellan, Copernicus, and Galileo did, to stand up for concepts often frowned upon in the working world and our modern society? How is it possible that these metaphysical concepts such as caring, compassion and love are keys to our personal and professional success?

* * *

The scientific method consists of the observation of the physical world, the formulation of theories (i.e., what does this observed data mean), and the task of conducting experiments to prove or disprove the assumptions and theories. While this basic definition of science has not changed over time, what constitutes valid and observable data has changed so much that the line between science and metaphysics no longer remains clear and distinct.

I will divide the accepted world of science into three categories. First, the physical sciences such as physics, chemistry and astronomy provide us with information about the "stuff" that makes up our universe. We know the elements that comprise matter, the makeup of planet and galaxies light-years from our home planet Earth, and many of the rules, such as the laws of thermal dynamics and gravity, that govern these bodies. Known as the hard sciences, these sciences are more black and white as the subjects under observation behave more or less the same in experiment after experiment. Combining two parts hydrogen with one part oxygen always results in water (H_2O). Logic, for the most part, rules the data found in the world of hard science.

Our biological sciences show how the basic building blocks of the physical sciences combine into living, breathing organisms. Living organisms do not always behave in the same predictable manner as our physical sciences. The behavior patterns are less predictable and less defined. While the use of penicillin to fight off a bacterial infection should work, there is no guarantee that a particular strain of bacteria has not mutated such that penicillin will no longer kill the bacteria. The strain may need another type of antibiotic, or it may have become immune to all known forms of antibiotics.

Lastly, our social sciences, such as psychology, sociology and anthropology, tell us about the individual and group behaviors of those living, breathing organisms described by our biological sciences. Our body of knowledge consists of trends and tendencies. One form of treatment may cure depression for one individual and have no effect on another. While our physical sciences denote hard observable behavior, our social sciences represent softer observed behavior. Logic no longer rules. Hunches, intuition and feelings begin playing more of a role in the application of these soft sciences.

As our scientific knowledge increases, the distinction between science and metaphysics blurs. Metaphysics constitute
the body of information and belief about existence and being, a body of knowledge not scientifically proven.
Previously, I gave an example of the numerous people who
had a near-death experience. Dr. Elisabeth Kübler-Ross interviewed some twenty thousand people who will swear there
is an afterlife. However, members of our medical profession
claim that the near-death experience does not prove the existence of an after-life. To them, the near-death experience
represents the natural and final shutdown of the brain at the
end of life. So who is right—those who died and returned to
tell of their experience and personal knowledge of the after-
life, or some of the medical community who claim that the
near-death experience is simply the last experience before the
void? No answer can be provided, either way, that can currently meet acceptable scientific criteria.

What then do we know about the near-death experience? We
know what people who have experienced death and returned
tell us. We know that we are likely to have a similar experience when we die. We know that when we have that
experience we will judge the success or failure of our lives
from the same perspective as those twenty thousand people
Dr. Elisabeth Kübler-Ross interviewed who had died and
come back to life: the perspective of how we have treated
others. Beyond this criterion that we will use to judge our
lives, we only know that an afterlife, or a void, is a matter of
belief, and not scientific proof.

However, scientific proof does not constitute the only source
of knowledge. There are things that we know are real, yet no

scientific proof exists. Take the concept of love. We all experience love during our lives, yet no scientific proof can be presented that verifies love is real. We do not look at love and claim it does not exist because it can't be proven. We know that it exists because we all experience it. Because something does not have scientific validation does not mean that it is not real. It only means that there is no scientific data to prove it is or is not real. We must be the final judge regarding whether we believe in love's existence and the role it will play in our lives.

* * *

Surprisingly, our scientific community has begun to validate some of the metaphysical concepts that so often give meaning to our lives. Consider the following three social science findings:

A 1972 study, which has been repeated numerous times, showed a measurable reduction in crime when only one percent of the population participated in the practice of meditation. Crime rates returned to normal when the meditative practices ceased.[34]

A 2001 pregnancy study of 219 women (ages 26 to 46) found that women were twice as likely to become pregnant if strangers prayed for them. The women did not know that strangers were praying for them. The women trying to conceive were treated at a fertilization clinic in Seoul, Korea, while the prayer groups were located in the United States, Canada, and Australia.[35]

The Research Center at the University of Michigan found a dramatic increase in the life expectancy of people who regularly performed volunteer work. [36]

Two of these scientific studies address meditation and prayer, both metaphysical concepts. The third shows longer life spans in people who perform volunteer work. None of these studies explains why prayer, meditation or volunteering works. While our social sciences are showing us the benefits and value of such activities as care, compassion and love, our biological and physical sciences, on the other hand, are providing new insight into and proof of how they work. For example, we now know that when an individual experiences positive emotions, the body produces more DHEA (the anti-aging hormone). Someone who does volunteer work for a cause in which he or she believes and freely gives time and energy tends to experience more positive emotions that cause the body to produce more of the anti-aging hormone DHEA. Thus, this person tends to live longer. By demonstrating that various metaphysical concepts do have tangible benefits, science is showing us that we can change the odds of our success and happiness.

The Myth of Working Hard

In the introduction, I established three traditional methods for success: working hard, working smart, and doing less to accomplish more. These methods are expressed in the concepts of effort, efficiency and effectiveness. Science provides some surprising insights into our traditional views of working hard and being smart.

Applying the rules of logic, it seems that if we work hard, then we should get more done. If we get more done, then we should be more successful. So why did John Gray, the author of *Men are From Mars, Women are from Venus,* find more personal and professional success when he stopped working hard and placed more emphasis on his relationship with his wife?

In the case of working hard, U.S. government studies reveal that working hard does not necessarily result in more work being performed. As discussed in the introduction, the trait known as the "fatigue factor" reveals that after working 60 hours per week for three months, the average weekly productivity drops to less than 20 hours for a full 60 hours of work—20 hours of productive work out of a 60-hour work-week! Mental and physical stress results in a greater number of mistakes, resulting in more rework. This, coupled with the need for more breaks and other factors, results in less work accomplished, not more. Corporate executives who push employees for extended periods would quickly find smarter ways to work if they realized that by working employees for extended periods, they actually accomplished less (and paid more) than if they worked normal hours.

When employees are pushed for extended periods, less work occurs. On the other hand, short, reasonable bursts of hard work often result in additional productivity. The trick lies in balancing shorter periods of working hard for a valid purpose with normal workloads that allow balance with our personal lives to occur. Notice that I said working hard for a valid purpose. Hard work applied in the wrong situation or toward the wrong end can demoralize a company.

Basic time management teaches us to create priority lists. Our high-priority A items should be addressed first thing in the morning, followed by priority B items and lastly by the lower priority C items. When we work hard at checking off our low priority C items because they are simple, yet fail to address the majority of our high-priority A items, we are less likely to accomplish our goals. Focusing on our high priority items (those things that are the most important to success) allows us to achieve our goals. Suppose your car needs gas and a car wash. Pressed for time, you stop at a service station. Do you buy gas or do you run your car through the automated car wash? Seems like a simple decision, yet in our lives we often work hard at the wrong things. Our goals are more likely to be realized if we create a strategy for what we should work on (our priority A items) and what we can let slip if needed (our priority C items).

At its simplest, strategy is about focusing on what is important. It's about doing the right thing. It's about centering our attention on those things that bring success. If something has to slip, let it be the non-important priority C item. Without a strategy, it becomes simple to get lost in the vast forest of priority C items.

The Myth of Being Smart

The fatigue factor shows that we cannot find success by continuing to trade hard work for valuable personal time needed to enjoy our families and lives. A logical alternative is to work smarter, not harder. We often, mistakenly, associate working smarter with that of being smart. Because the Western perspective places great emphasis on science and logic, we believe that smart people are more likely to be successful. Yet, the simple axiom that high IQ means success belongs in the same category as that of the Earth being flat or being the center of the Universe.

In 1985, Howard Gardner's *Frames of Mind* established the concept of multiple intelligences. Showing intelligence to be more complex than mere intellect, Gardner established various types of intelligence: logical-mathematical, musical, spatial, bodily / kinesthetic, knowing how to deal with others, and how to deal with ourselves.[37]

John Mayer and Peter Salovey would later create the theory of "emotional intelligence" that defines our ability to recognize and manage emotions.[38] However, it was not until 1996, when Daniel Goleman published his book, *Emotional Intelligence*, that the world finally sat up and took notice. Doc Childre and Howard Martin indicate in their book *The HeartMath Solution* that Goleman's findings clearly show:

Success in all areas of our lives is based more on the ability to recognize and manage emotions than on our IQ and it explains why many average IQ individuals routinely outperform higher IQ individuals.[39]

Research shows that IQ is not as much a factor in determining success as we think. Goleman referenced numerous studies confirming the lack of a strong link between IQ and success. [40] For example, one study of ninety-five Harvard graduates from the 1940s found that by middle age, the top graduates were no more successful than other lower-scoring Harvard graduates, not in their professional careers (money, title, contributions, etc.) nor in their personal lives (happiness, relationships, family, etc.).[41]

Goleman referenced a study of 450 boys from the same socioeconomic rank and geographic location that found that by middle age, seven percent of those with IQs below 80 had been unemployed for at least 10 years. However, so had seven percent of those with IQs above 100. The study concluded that traits we now associate with emotional intelligence seemed to have a greater influence on those who had achieved success.[42]

Consider the study Goleman referenced of 81 salutatorians and valedictorians from the 1981 Illinois high school graduating classes. Although these students had graduating at the top of their classes, ten years later just one out of four excelled in their professions when compared to other similar-aged graduates. Most had achieved only average levels of success.[43]

* * *

Do not assume that intelligence implies failure. This is faulty logic. Research shows that IQ simply does not have a strong correlation to success or failure. Whereas emotional intelligence strongly correlates to success in both the personal and professional arenas, IQ shows no correlation. It plays no role either way. A better view of IQ places it in the same domain as our other God-given skills: physical skills for athletes, verbal skills for speakers, or music skills for performing arts, etc. Our intelligence quotient represents a valuable skill and should be appreciated and applied whenever possible.

The amazing aspect about emotional intelligence is that, unlike IQ, it is not fixed. It can be developed and matured.

> *Unlike IQ, emotional intelligence is not fixed.*
> *It can be developed and matured.*

Our emotional intelligence most strongly correlates to success. We have the ability to increase and mature our emotional intelligence; so what exactly is the key to emotional intelligence?

Goleman says that the key to emotional intelligence is being aware of our feelings when they occur.[44] Only when we become aware of our emotions are we capable of managing them. However, managing emotions does not mean not having emotions. Nor does it mean being in control of your emotions. Managing your emotions means becoming aware of them at an appropriate stage so you can respond appropriately.

Ronald Reagan was a master of emotional management. His wife Nancy talked about how the President managed the emotions of those around him. [45] President Reagan used his humor and story-telling abilities to bring his cabinet members back to a calmer frame of mind when he saw emotions teetering on the verge of affecting matters of national consequences. Amidst heated discussions, cabinet members would suddenly find the President discussing an event from the President's childhood—maybe a story about saving a cow on the farm—that brought laughter and amusement to the staff. Once the President had lowered the emotional intensity, he would direct the conversation back to our nation's business. President Reagan was able to sense the emotional mood of a meeting and then easily manage it.

Our most harmful emotions are the negative ones. For example, consider the emotion of anger. There are varying degrees of anger ranging from a mild form, irritation, to its most severe form, fury. The spectrum of anger consists of irritation, annoyance, anger, rage and fury. Emotional management is simply having the ability to become aware of our emotions and take actions based on them before severe consequences result. The sooner we become aware that something is irritating or annoying us, the sooner we can act and resolve the situation without serious ramifications. However, if we let our emotions reach the stage of fury, our actions and the resulting consequences could be dramatic and serious.

The five basic emotions are anger, fear, sadness, guilt, and happiness. The following graphic illustrates three basic negative emotions and their associated scales:

Anger	Fear	Sadness
Fury	Terror	Suicide
Rage	Panic	Gloom
Anger	Horror	Grief
Annoyance	Fear	Misery
Irritation	Alarm	Sorrow
	Trepidation	Sadness
	Apprenhension	Melancholy

If we are melancholy or sad, the sooner we take action to re-solve our feelings, the less likely we are to progress to the harsher states of misery, gloom or suicide. Too often, we hear of the murder of a spouse due to emotions getting out of hand during an argument. According to an FBI study, these so-called crimes of passion constitute the largest per-cent of all murders.[46] A jealous ex-boyfriend who cannot move on with his life kills the new boyfriend or his ex-girlfriend. When we are unaware of emotions or when they are left unchecked, serious and sometimes irreparable conse-quences occur. Yet our emotions remain our most vital sensing mechanism for what is happening to us. Our emotions are the doorways to managing our lives.

- We are irritated—why? What is causing the irritation? What do we need to do to resolve the irritation so that it does not progress to anger or fury?

- We are sad—why? What is causing us to be sad and what must we do to move on? What do we need to change in our lives?

Emotional management occurs when we learn how to recognize and be in touch with our emotions. We cannot manage something of which we are unaware. How do we learn to manage our emotions? An examination of how our emotions work not only reveals how we can better manage our emotions, but it also uncovers the secrets of heart / brain entrainment and the key to a successful life.

How Our Emotions Work

Inside the brain, the amygdala assigns emotional significance to the things we perceive though our senses.[47] For many years, scientists believed that the information we perceived from our five senses went first to the thalamus, which then passed the information to the cerebral cortex for analysis. This transmission occurred before the information reached the amygdala for emotional evaluation. However, neuroscientists have discovered that this scientific theory is incorrect. In reality, our sensory input goes to the amygdala for emotional assessment and action *before* reaching the cerebral cortex for rational decision-making.[48]

Old Theory of Emotional Evaluation

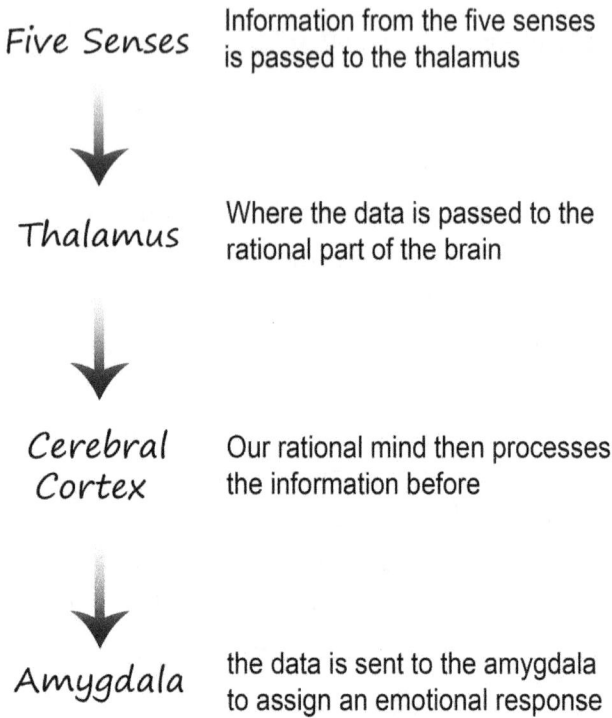

Five Senses   Information from the five senses is passed to the thalamus

↓

Thalamus   Where the data is passed to the rational part of the brain

↓

Cerebral Cortex   Our rational mind then processes the information before

↓

Amygdala   the data is sent to the amygdala to assign an emotional response

New research shows a more complicated path in which the rational mind receives the data *after* the emotional response occurs.

Our Emotional Response Actually Occurs *Before* Rational Processing

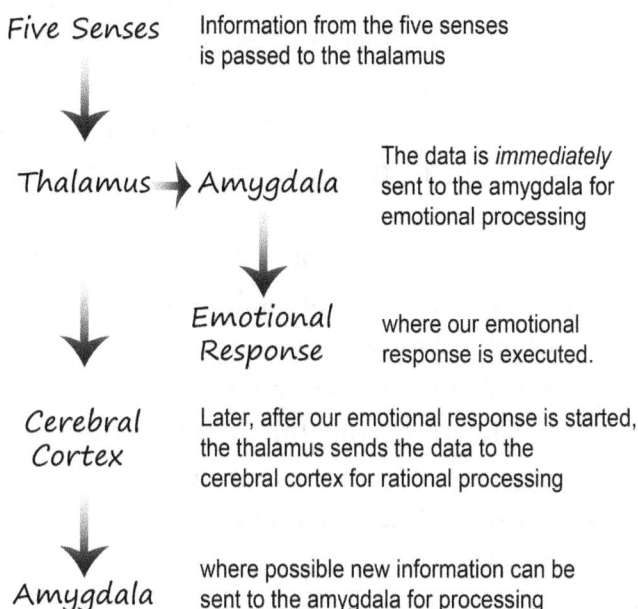

Five Senses — Information from the five senses is passed to the thalamus

↓

Thalamus ➔ Amygdala — The data is *immediately* sent to the amygdala for emotional processing

↓

Emotional Response — where our emotional response is executed.

Cerebral Cortex — Later, after our emotional response is started, the thalamus sends the data to the cerebral cortex for rational processing

↓

Amygdala — where possible new information can be sent to the amygdala for processing

In other words, our emotional responses occur before we have time to think about them. For example, a dog bites Amanda as a small child while she is walking past a lavender bush. As an adult, she passes a lavender bush, immediately tenses and becomes afraid.

Amanda's brain, as she passes the lavender bush, senses the lavender scent and sends that information to the thalamus, which immediately forwards the information to the amygdala for emotional processing. The amygdala searches for past memories of lavender. It quickly finds the dog-biting incident and immediately executes commands in response to our basic flight or fight instincts. She tenses and becomes afraid.

97

As Amanda's emotional reaction of fear occurs, the thalamus is sending her sensory information to the cerebral cortex for rational processing. Amanda soon realizes that the real threat is dogs, not lavender. She surveys the neighborhood and sees no dogs or other possible threats. She relaxes and continues her stroll. Only after her emotional response is well underway does the thalamus send the sensory information to Amanda's cerebral cortex for rational decision making. The rational analysis performed by her cerebral cortex overrides her original emotional response; only after the emotional response has occurred does she realize that there is no danger present. This same type of processing occurs when we find ourselves saying things in the heat of the situation that we later wish we had never said. Our awareness of our emotions can at times occur after lasting and sometimes permanent damage occurs.

Amanda's reactions when walking past a lavender bush consisted of two different responses. Her first reaction of fear corresponds to our basic *fight or flight* survival instincts, which are located in the area of the brain known as the reptilian brain. Her second reaction of calm after realizing that there was nothing to fear comes from our *foresight* ability to analyze and problem solve. This ability lies in a separate part of the brain known as the cerebral cortex. Two different parts of the brain trigger Amanda's two reactions.

Surprisingly, initial processing for each of her reactions occurred in a third and very separate part of the brain, the emotional component, which contains the amygdala, known as the limbic system. Before Amanda's *fight or flight* response occurred or before her *foresight* processing occurred, the emotional center of the brain first processed the information about the lavender bush. Our emotional brain makes the first assessment of all situations in which we find ourselves. Thus, our emotional part of the brain is a critical element in our basic survival and everyday functioning. Let's take a closer look at how our brain works.

The Triune Brain

Scientists today recognize three distinct and separate areas of the brain. Known as the triune brain, each area corresponds to a unique responsibility or processing capability.

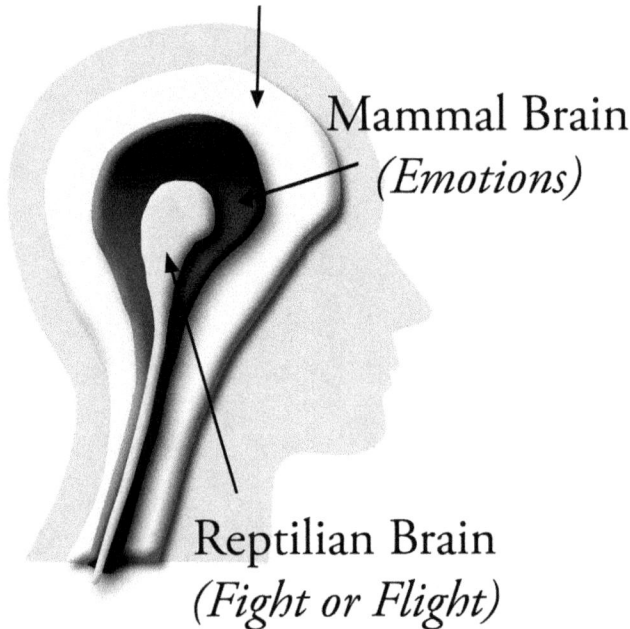

Primate Brain
(Foresight)

Mammal Brain
(Emotions)

Reptilian Brain
(Fight or Flight)

The reptilian brain, found at the base or center of the brain, controls our basic survival activities: hunger, thirst, temperature control, hormones, approach, avoidance, heart rate, reproduction, etc. It is often characterized as the part of the brain that controls our *fight or flight* activities. Called the reptilian brain, or R-Complex (R for reptilian), it has survival characteristics similar to the brains of reptiles such as snakes and lizards. The reptilian brain is the first part of the brain to develop in a fetus.

Animals such as dogs and cats demonstrate emotions such as anger, fear, maternal love, social bonding and jealousy. Our limbic system, or mammal brain, is similar to the brains of dogs and cats. The limbic system, also known as the emotional brain, is wrapped around the reptilian brain.

Lastly, wrapped around the emotional brain, the neocortex or primate brain controls our foresight abilities: problem solving, self-reflection, self-awareness, advanced planning and ability to choose appropriate behavior, etc. Characterized as our *foresight* abilities, the human primate brain is much larger than the cortexes of other primates such as monkeys or chimpanzees.

	Name	Location	Characteristics
The Thinking Brain	Neocortex known as the Primate Brain	Outer part of the brain	*Foresight* activities found in humans
The Emotional Brain	Limbic System known as the Mammal Brain	Middel part of the brain	*Emotional* capabilities found in dogs, cats, bears, and lions
The Reptilian Brain (Flight or Flight)	R-Complex known as the Reptilian Brain	Innermost part of the brain (brain stem)	*Fight or Flight* activities found in reptiles such as snakes, crocodiles, lizards, and turtles

* * *

New research shows that whereas our reptilian brain controls our *fight or flight* activities and our primate brain controls our *foresight* abilities, the emotional brain acts as a switch, directing our energy to the reptilian brain or to the primate brain.

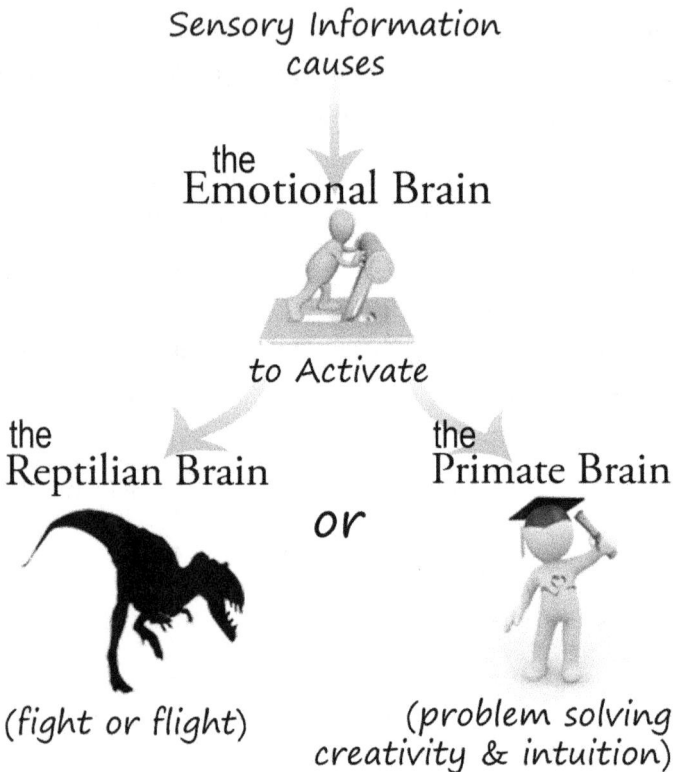

Sensory Information
causes

the
Emotional Brain

to Activate

the
Reptilian Brain

or

the
Primate Brain

(fight or flight)

(problem solving
creativity & intuition)

Our Emotional Brain Acts As A Switch That
Activates Either Our Reptilian or Our Primate Brain

* * *

The transmission in an automobile allows the energy from the engine to move the car in either a forward direction or a reverse direction—depending on whether we have placed the gearshift in forward or reverse. Likewise, the emotional brain directs our brain energy to be applied in either its *fight or flight* regions or its *foresight* regions. We can easily control our emotional brain to shift our energy forward into our *foresight* regions or backwards into our *fight or flight* activities as will be discussed later in this book.

The average person's *fight or flight* reptilian brain consumes 65% of the brain's total energy. When we learn to shift our brain's energy away from the *fight or flight* reptilian brain and to our *foresight* primate brain, we enhance and heighten our problem solving, creative, decision making, and intuitive abilities. How could we fail to be more successful in our lives if we transition out of our *fight or flight* areas of the brain and into our *foresight* areas of the brain?

* * *

Paralleling our reptilian brain and our primate brain are two subsystems of the autonomic nervous system (ANS): the sympathetic nervous system and the parasympathetic nervous system.

The sympathetic nervous system, associated with our *fight or flight* reptilian brain, prepares the body for *action* by performing such functions as increasing heart rate, dilating bronchioles for more oxygen, secreting adrenaline, stopping digestion and dilating pupils.

On the other hand, the parasympathetic nervous system, associated with our primate brain, prepares the body for *foresight* activities by performing such functions as decreasing heart rate, constricting bronchioles, constricting pupils, and allowing digestion.

When we face danger, our energy diverts to our *fight or flight* systems by means of the reptilian brain and the sympathetic nervous system. Digestion stops, diverting energy to our muscles for running. Our bronchioles dilate so we can absorb more oxygen.

When we need to solve problems, the opposite occurs. Our energy diverts to our *foresight* systems by means of the primate brain and the parasympathetic nervous system.

Not only does our emotional brain act as a switch for the reptilian and primate brains, it also indirectly acts as a switch for the sympathetic and parasympathetic nervous systems that control the energy throughout our entire body.

Sensory Information
causes

the
Emotional Brain

to Activate

the
Reptilian Brain

the
Primate Brain

or

Sympathetic
Nervous System

Parasympathetic
Nervous System

Our Emotional Brain Acts as a Switch That Activates Either Our Entire
Fight or Flight Subsystem or Our Foresight Subsystem within the Body

We can now see how critical emotional intelligence is to success. Our emotional center controls and directs our actions. It directs our energy to exercise either our *foresight* capabilities or our *fight or flight* activities. Since we spend the majority of our time and energy dwelling in our *fight or flight* systems, it only makes sense that if we learn how to shift our energy to our *foresight* systems, we increase our odds of success. The key lies in finding out how we can gain more control over the switch (the emotional brain) that directs our energy.

Controlling the Switch

In the emotional brain, the amygdala assigns emotional significance to our sensory input.[49] Research proves the amygdala in the emotional brain is the switch that activates different areas of the brain. Neuroscientists found heightened activity in the foresight primate brain when they stimulated the front part of the amygdala. Conversely, they found heightened fight or flight activities in the reptilian brain when they stimulated the rear part of the amygdala.

Unfortunately, neuroscientists cannot electrically probe us whenever we feel the need to activate a certain part of our brain. Other research, however, has uncovered how we can gain control over this valuable switching mechanism in the brain.

* * *

In 1991, Doc Childre spearheaded the foundation of the Institute of HeartMath. This non-profit institute of research and education focuses on the fields of neuroscience, cardiology, psychology, physiology, biochemistry, bioelectricity and physics.[50]

In 1999, Doc Childre and Howard Martin published *The Heartmath Solution*, describing the next evolution in understanding intelligence. Pioneers such as Howard Gardner, John Mayer, Peter Salovey and Daniel Goleman dismantled our definition of intelligence, replacing it with a more comprehensive and predictable definition of intelligence as it relates to success. The Institute of HeartMath adds to that definition and provides the missing link, showing what makes it all work.

In his book *Brain and Perception*, Dr. Karl Pribram explains that the amygdala's job is to compare new data with familiar emotional memories.[51] This is why we often respond to new situations with the emotions that do not always makes sense[52] We saw a brief example of this phenomenon in our example of Amanda and her fearful reaction to a lavender bush because, as a child, a dog bit her near a lavender bush.

However, the amygdala and its response (along with the thalamus and the cortex[53]) is also influenced by another organ—the heart.[54]

Heart Intelligence

We are all familiar with the concept that the brain is the master. It alone acts as the commander-in-chief, sending messages obeyed by the various parts of the body. This concept, actually, is relatively new in the overall history of humankind. While the Egyptians removed the internal organs (including the brain) when preparing the dead for their travels to the afterlife, they left the heart intact within the chest cavity, feeling that the heart would be needed in the afterlife. The Egyptians were not alone in this view of the importance of the heart. The Greeks, Babylonians, and Mesopotamians all maintained the importance of the heart's influence on our lives: our emotions, our decision-making, even our morality. [55]

Traditional Chinese Medicine (TCM), a practice of balancing the energy of the organs in the body, considers the heart to be the most crucial organ within the body and gives it the name, "the Emporia." Other ancient teachings also stress the importance of the heart.

Modern science is providing evidence that the teachings of the ancients may not be as naïve as we believed—the heart may be more than a simple pump controlled by the brain. For example, in an unborn fetus, the heart automatically starts beating before there is a brain—proving that the brain does not control the beating of the heart as previously thought.[56] The brain develops in stages: first the brainstem, then the emotional regions of the brain, and lastly, the rational thinking brain. However, there is a beating heart before there is a brain.[57]

Additional evidence comes from information that we have learned from heart transplants, which dispels the notion that the brain controls the beating of the heart by means of the autonomic nervous system. During a heart transplant, surgeons sever the nerves connecting the brain and the heart with no known method to reconnect them. Yet once the heart is shocked into beating, it beats for a lifetime without any physical connection to brain.[58]

The heart also seems to have a mind of its own. In the 1970s, physiologists John and Beatrice Lacey provided evidence that the heart does in fact behave as if it has a mind of its own—quite the opposite of the heart simply obeying the brain's messages sent via our nervous system. The Laceys found that arousal signals sent from the brain to the heart and other organs generally caused the heartbeat to speed up while the other organs responded accordingly. However, sometimes the heart would slow down rather than speed up. The other organs continued to respond normally to the arousal signal. The heart behaved independent of the brain's commands. It makes up its own mind as to whether it will comply or not. However, more information surfaced.

The Laceys discovered the heart actually responds to the brain by sending messages of its own—messages that the brain understands and obeys. The idea that the heart is a mechanical organ controlled by the brain is no longer the case. Rather, the heart is an independent organ, having its own agenda in influencing the behavior of a person.[59]

Neuroscientists added to the groundwork provided by the Laceys by uncovering an independent nervous system within the heart, complete with neurons and transmissions to and from the brain.[60] We now know that the heart communicates with the brain and the body in four ways to exert its influence:

- Neurologically: nerve impulses
- Biochemically: hormones and neurotransmitters
- Biophysically: pressure waves
- Energetically: electromagnetic field interaction[61]

Today it is accepted that the heart has a mind of its own. In 1991, Dr. J. Andrew Armour provided evidence "of a functional *heart brain*". [62] Dr. Armour showed a sophisticated system within the heart consisting of neurotransmitters, neurons, support cells and proteins that allow the heart to act independently from the brain. [63] When we combine the research of our social and medical sciences, a clearer picture emerges of how our heart, brain, and body work together.

* * *

Among the messages sent by the heart to the brain are those directed to the emotional brain, specifically to the amygdala, the switch that activates either our *foresight* or *flight or fight* responses. Much like the neuroscientists who electrically stimulated either the front or rear part of the amygdala causing activity in either our primate or our reptilian brain, messages from the heart also stimulate either the front or rear part of amygdala, thereby triggering activity in the fore-sight primate brain or fight or flight activity in the reptilian brain.

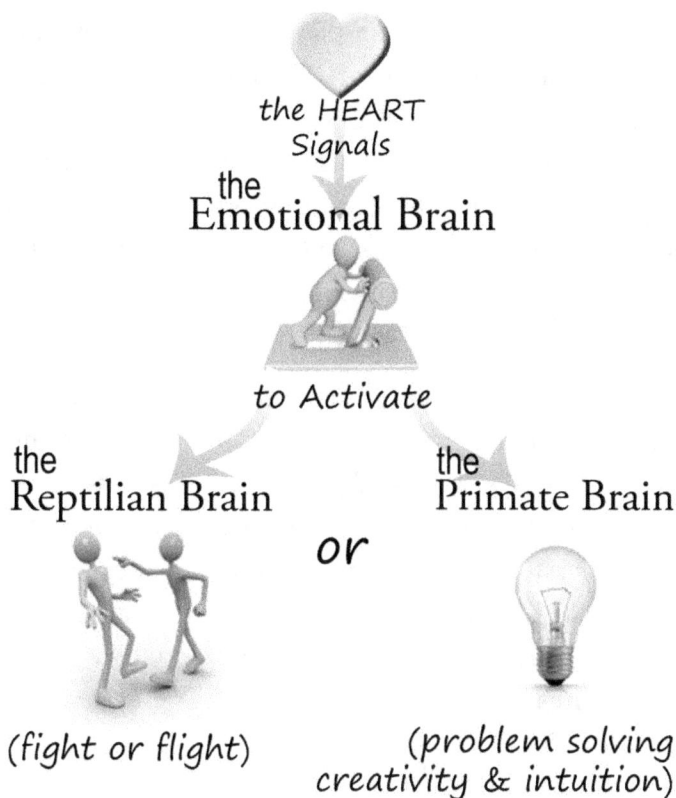

the HEART
Signals

the
Emotional Brain

to Activate

the
Reptilian Brain

or

the
Primate Brain

(fight or flight)

(problem solving
creativity & intuition)

The Heart Influences the Amygdala in Our Emotional Brain -- the Switch for Our Flight or Flight Subsystem or Our Foresight Subsystem

The research of Doc Childre, Howard Martin and the Institute of HeartMath is proving that "heart intelligence actually transfers intelligence to the emotions and instills the power of emotional management. In other words, heart intelligence is really the source of emotional intelligence."[64] With the discovery of a *heart brain*, a new type of intelligence emerges—heart intelligence.

* * *

How do we translate this knowledge into everyday successful living? The answer, based on the defined hierarchy of intelligences, is to develop our heart intelligence so the emotional brain and rational brain work in harmony with the heart. Since the heart can stimulate the amygdala in the emotional brain, which in turn activates either our reptilian or primate brain, the most effect is achieved by applying the intelligence that has the most control over our results—heart intelligence.

Just as *attitude* (that determines *behavior* that determines *consequences*) is the means to affect the most with the least effort, so too is heart intelligence the means to affect the most with the least effort. This may be hard to accept, but it is the cornerstone to creating a successful life. How do we develop heart intelligence? It turns out that heart intelligence is the easiest of all intelligences to develop. The secret to a successful life lies in its simplicity.

Activating Heart / Brain Entrainment

When subjects were hooked up to instruments measuring brain waves and heart rate variability (i.e., the rate at which heart rate changes over time) it was found heart / brain entrainment was easily induced—or reversed. The Institute of Heartmath found that in order to induce entrainment, subjects needed only to focus their attention in their heart region and recall feelings of love, appreciation and caring (i.e., positive feelings).

Positive feelings reduce the production of cortisol (a stress hormone) while increasing the production of both DHEA (the anti-aging hormone) and IgA (an antibody used in the immune system), as well as reducing blood pressure.[65] People who perform volunteer work tend to live longer simply because their volunteer work creates positive feelings, thereby lowering stress, increasing the production of the anti-aging hormone, and strengthening the immune system. It is only logical that they would live longer.

However, research shows that feelings of anger, fear, frustration, etc., create disharmony between the brain and the heart—overall effectiveness (physical, mental and emotional) decreases.

* * *

When we create positive feelings, we induce heart / brain entrainment and thereby heighten our *foresight* abilities. In essence, the heart (via positive emotions) throws the switch (stimulates the amygdala in the emotional brain) thereby directing energy and activity in our primate brain and parasympathetic nervous system; thereby heightening our problem solving, creativity, decision making, etc.

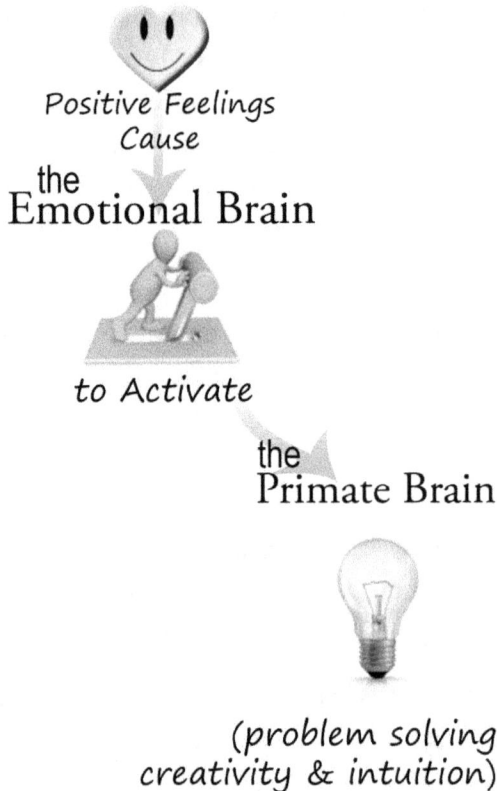

Positive Feelings
Cause
the
Emotional Brain

to Activate

the
Primate Brain

(problem solving creativity & intuition)

Positive Feelings Stimulate the Front Part of the Amygdala --Thereby Activating Our "Foresight" Subsystem Within the Body

On the other hand, when we experience negative feelings, we take ourselves out of a state of heart / brain entrainment and heighten our *fight or flight* abilities, redirecting valuable energy away from our *foresight* capacities. In essence, the heart (through negative emotions) stimulates the rear part of the amygdala in the emotional brain, activating more energy and activity in our reptilian brain and sympathetic nervous system and thereby reducing our problem solving, creativity, decision making, etc.

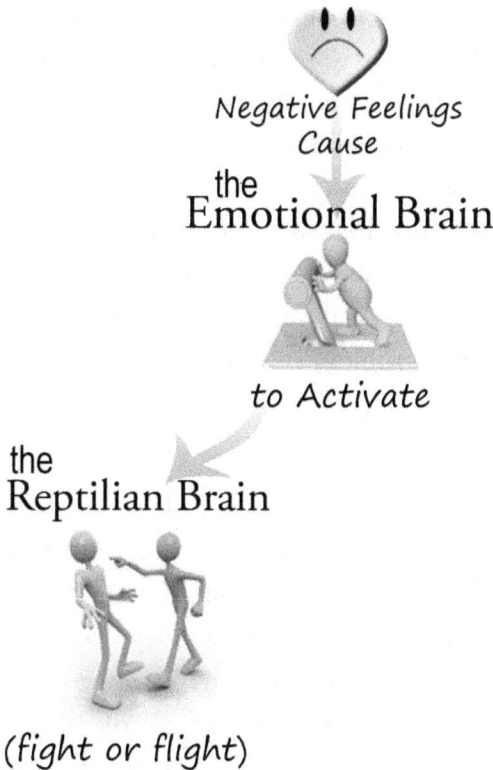

Negative Feelings Cause

the
Emotional Brain

to Activate

the
Reptilian Brain

(fight or flight)

Negative Feelings Stimulate the Rear Part of the Amygdala --Thereby Activating Our "Fight or Flight" Subsystem Within the Body

* * *

Donald from hospice told me about all the caring he saw as he faced the end of his life, the same caring described in the Hawthorne Effect and the same caring that induces heart / brain entrainment that places us in an optimal state to succeed. Donald wasn't alone in his advice from the dying. Thomas (a president of a corporation), Jonathan (a hat maker), Mary (an artist), Ellen (a factory worker), John (a train conductor), William (a program manager), Sally (a real estate agent)—the list goes on and on, from presidents to janitors—all told me in their own way that it is our relationships with others that is our real work in life. Work is something you do to make a living, they said, but the people in your life are where one finds or loses true riches. According to the dying, choose love and you will die a happier person. According to science, choose love and you optimize the chances of being successful because you actually increase your decision-making, problem solving, creativity and intuitive skills.

* * *

When I decided to take a risk and choose love, to start placing relationships and the way I treated others at the top of my priority list, I did not know about the discoveries by Howard Garner, John Mayer, Peter Salovey, Daniel Goleman, Doc Childre, Howard Martin, Karl Pribram, John and Beatrice Lacey, Andrew Armour, and a host of other scientists. I knew my dilemma seemed similar to that of most people trying to get ahead in the world. I could listen to my head—after all, I had done OK in my career, not so great in my marriage, but the majority of the Western world was be-

hind me—or listen to my heart and what the dying were saying, take a chance and maybe discover the real meaning of
life.

Dr. Elisabeth Kübler-Ross and my own findings at hospice
ended the debate:

> "The dying learn a great deal at the end of life, usually
> when it is too late to apply."[66]

When I made a decision to listen to my heart and place caring, compassion, and the way I treated people at the
forefront of my corporate behavior, I unknowingly began
shifting my energy out of my reptilian brain and into my
primate brain. By focusing on how I treated people, I felt better about myself. I had more feelings of caring and
compassion towards the people with whom I worked. Not
only did I have more feelings that were positive, but those
around me also felt better because of how I was treating
them. I not only created a state of heart / brain entrainment
in myself more often, but I was creating a state of heart /
brain entrainment in those around me. We were now working out of our primate brains more frequently. We were
working from a state of heightened creativity, problem solving, decision-making, and intuitive abilities. How could we
help but be more successful at whatever we were attempting
to accomplish?

* * *

Unpeel the layers on John Gray's story and you find a similar
tale. The author of *Men are From Mars, Women are from
Venus* began to allocate an hour each day to his wife and one
less hour to his work. Because of his focus on his wife, his

relationship with her became better. A better spousal relationship created feelings that were more positive; more positive feelings created heart / brain entrainment, thereby heightening his *foresight* abilities. With better problem solving skills, creativity and intuition, John Gray tilted the odds of success in his favor. Consequently, he became even more successful at his work.

John Gray and I both found success by unknowingly applying the entrainment factor in our lives. When we look closely, we find the entrainment factor at the center of many successes. We have already discussed how many of today's motivation techniques have at their basis the "Hawthorne Effect"—the concept that productivity and motivation increase when workers feel cared about by their management. Caring creates positive emotions, which places people in states of entrainment.

Demonstrably better learning occurs when students engage in "participative learning," a style of education in which students are involved in the learning experience. Think about the last seminar or lecture you attended. Did the person engage you in one form or another? Did they use jokes, tell touching stories or have activities for you to participate in to assist them in conveying their message, or did they methodically go about presenting only the facts? Which style do you remember best and from which one did you learn more? Participative learning proves far more effective as a teaching approach because at its heart is the concept of entrainment. When someone tells a joke, or a touching story, or gets you involved in an activity, you unknowingly experience positive feelings. Those positive feelings get you out of your reptilian brain and into your foresight brain—exactly where you need to be for effective learning to occur. The opposite happens from the boring lecturer who almost puts you to sleep with his or her presentation of fact after boring fact. This dry communication of information has no chance of reaching in, grabbing you, and creating positive feelings, thereby pulling you out of your reptilian brain and into your foresight brain. Peeling away the layers, we see entrainment beams out from successful techniques in all areas of life.

The Meaning of Entrainment

What does it all mean? It means the real purpose in our lives, the real way our body, mind and heart work most efficiently, revolves around the heart and feelings of caring, appreciation, and love—those things we were taught as children. Whether we listen to our scientists and their new understanding of emotional and heart intelligence, or to the dying, the message is loud and clear: compassion, love and caring are the keys to a successful life.

Positive feelings create states of efficiency, better solutions and higher states of awareness. They create an environment in which success happens more naturally, with less effort and with more ease. Love, caring and compassion create positive emotions that are the key to creating a successful life.

Our *attitude* determines the *behavior* that causes the *consequences*.

Science now shows us the attitude that we learned from the dying in Section 1 is the right *attitude*:

> Attitudes of love, caring and compassion determine the behavior that causes the consequences that lead to a successful life.

* * *

With the knowledge that positive feelings create heart / brain entrainment, are you willing to start making the choices to tilt the odds of success in your favor? Choosing to create positive feelings in oneself and those around you not only creates the optimal environment for success, but it also makes the world a better place in which to live, much like Walt Disney's purpose to *make people happy.*

The fundamental key, the strategy to starting a more successful life, is simple—start making choices that create positive feelings. Change your life by implementing a simple strategy that provides you with better decision-making, problem solving, creative and intuitive skills.

You will find that as you choose to create positive feelings in your life a daily habit, you also begin the process of increasing your emotional intelligence. As you become more conscious of your choices, and how they affect your feelings, you address the fundamental key to maturing your emotional intelligence—being aware of your emotions. The earlier you recognize an emotion, the easier and quicker it is to manage that emotion. Addressing irritation is much easier than dealing with anger, which is much easier than dealing with fury or rage. We become proactive in managing our emotions, our success and our happiness. We start the process of being able to recognize issues when they are minute rather than when they have developed into trouble and sickness. We start applying the concept of doing less and accomplishing more, as illustrated by the three physicians:

> The eldest physician removes sickness when it is still spirit. As a result, his name is not heard outside the house.

The elder physician sees sickness while it is small, so he is known only in the neighborhood.

I massage skin and give herbs after sickness is easily recognized. Hence, I am widely known among the poor and the rich.[67]

Over time, we learn to live in harmony with our emotions, our feelings, our work, and our personal lives. We find the spirit of joyful living, and the heart is where we find it.

Principle 2: Strategy

At the beginning of this section, I related a story of two people traveling to a foreign country seeking answers and receiving two beautiful birds as gifts. These birds, they believed, could potentially help them find the answers they sought. Years later, the old grandfather, who gave the strangers these birds, visited his pupils only to find two very different results. One had found happiness and comfort in the bird they kept caged, but had not found abundance. The other, filled with compassion, gave her bird freedom. As a result, she found great abundance. The man and the woman chose different approaches regarding the gift they received from the old man, and each approach produced a different result. It is our *approach* to our lives, relationships and chosen professions that determines our odds of finding happiness and reaching our goals. In order to accomplish our purpose, be it a life purpose, a business or professional purpose, or a personal purpose, it is critical that we establish a strategy to fulfill that purpose.

Examine these two purposes and strategies from Mary Kay and Walt Disney:

Mary Kay:

Purpose: "To give unlimited opportunity to women"[68]

Strategy: Create a cosmetics-based company in which women can excel

Walt Disney:

Purpose: "To make people happy"[69]

Strategy: Through the media of entertainment, provide products (movies, TV, theme parks, etc.) that enrich and promote family values

As a child, I enjoyed with tremendous laughter the famous TV comedian Red Skelton. Red and Walt Disney had similar purposes in life—to make people happy. Each took a different strategy. Walt made movies and theme parks. Red told jokes, often bursting with laughter before he could complete the punch line. While each had a similar purpose, each followed a different strategy to accomplish his purpose based on his skills and passion.

Red Skelton did not focus on taking breathtaking photographs like Ansel Adams or composing moving music like Beethoven. Walt Disney did not try to finance loans so people could enjoy owning their own homes. Mary Kay did not start an automobile company, but rather based her strategy on what most women are taught as young girls—cosmetics. They established a strategy based on their individual skills and passions giving them the best means to fulfill their stated purpose.

Passion and Skills

A strategy should accomplish three things. First, it should align itself with your purpose. Second, it should reflect your passion and skills. Third, it should serve as a guiding light or beacon by which you make decisions.

Section 1 taught us our life purpose—to learn about and practice love. Our life strategy should align itself with our life purpose, as there are many ways to learn about and practice love. Fortunately, our life purpose is encoded into the very existence of humankind. It is almost impossible for someone to survive an earthly existence without learning about love and loving people around him or her. Woven into the very fabric of life, it is impossible to avoid our life purpose. We can only accomplish it with different degrees of proficiency. However, we can choose a strategy by which to live our lives that enriches our lives rather than following a strategy that creates difficulty and hardship in our lives.

Our understanding of heart / brain entrainment shows that the best way to tilt the odds of creating success in our lives is to create positive feelings. When we create positive feelings, our heart triggers the front part of the amygdala, which activates our *foresight* capabilities in our brains. Positive feelings enhance our problem solving skills, creativity, intuition, decision-making abilities, etc. They place us in the optimal state for a successful life to occur with the least effort on our part. Common sense tells us our life strategy should be to create positive feelings.

The more positive feelings we create in our lives and those around us, the more we shift our energy to our *foresight* abilities and away from our *fight or flight* abilities, creating the optimal state for success to occur.

LIFE PRINCIPLES

Life Purpose: To learn and practice love

Life Strategy: Create positive feelings in ourselves and others

* * *

In order to fulfill our purpose, be it our life, personal, or professional purpose, we should choose a strategy that expresses our passion. Emotion comes from that about which we are passionate. Whenever our emotions rise, something has touched a part of us about which we care deeply. Anger rises because we feel someone has treated us or someone else unjustly. If we did not feel that an injustice occurred or if we did not care, we would not become emotional. If we did not care about justice in a particular situation, then anger would not flow forth from our heart.

I buy flowers for my wife because my love for her seeks expression. Whether it is positive or negative feelings that spring up in our lives, those feelings find expression through our emotions. The things about which we care feed, nourish, and give rise to creation, manifestation, and expression in the physical realm. Walt Disney loved kids and art; thus, he created cartoons. John Grey, the author of *Men are From*

Mars, Women are From Venus, loved his wife; hence, he placed her ahead of his work and as a result both his relationship and his work flourished.

Passion excites our motivation, fuels our energy, and drives our direction. Without passion, we are aimless in our direction. Without passion, we are much more likely to stray from our path. It only makes sense that our strategy should reflect that about which we are passionate. Red Skelton wanted to make people happy. His passion was in jokes, not in music or technology—both viable means to bring happiness to people.

In his national bestseller *Good to Great—Why Some Companies Make the Leap...and Others Don't,* Jim Collins states that passion is a necessary component for achieving greatness.[70] Collins astutely observes that to achieve greatness, you do not create passion—you discover what makes you passionate[71]. Walt Disney discovered his passion; Red Skelton discovered his; Mary Kay discovered hers; I have discovered mine, and whether you want to create abundance in your personal or professional lives, you must discover yours to help create a simple strategy to fulfill your personal or career purpose.

Passion, like energy, exists in two forms: kinetic and potential. Kinetic energy is energy in motion. What we already are passionate about is kinetic passion. What we do in our free time, what we read about or study, what we dream about— these are all indicators of things in which we are already interested and about which we have passion.

Potential energy is energy at rest, and so is potential passion. Unlimited opportunities are in the world. Sometimes we need to take action, expand our awareness, and experience things outside our current realm to find new passions. Whether we already know what we are passionate about or whether we need to expand our experiences to discover our passion, we must find our real interests, our passions, in order to develop a guiding strategy; it is no surprise that a key to a successful strategy, our passion, comes from the heart.

* * *

In *Good to Great,* Collins points out that great companies do not hide from reality, or as Collins puts it, they face the "brutal facts".[72] You must combine your passion with your skills. To do otherwise ignores the brutal facts.

Music is one of my hobbies. It is an interest, but certainly not something about which I can get passionate. Even in the category of hobby, I had to confront the brutal fact that I cannot sing--I do not possess a voice that produces pleasant melodies. However, I do have great hand-eye coordination and I am highly creative. Confronting the brutal facts, I realized that singing is not a strategy that allows me to enjoy, share and succeed in a musical hobby. Since I have good hand-eye coordination and creativity, playing an instrument such as the guitar allows me to create music and write my own songs, something I have enjoyed for over 20 years. It is a successful hobby because I confronted the brutal fact that I cannot sing, but am quite capable of playing an instrument and writing songs.

Kelly Tilghman loved golf. She grew up with golf—for 22 years her family owned and operated a golf course near Myrtle Beach, S.C. Kelly learned to play the game well enough to earn a scholarship to Duke University, winning the 1990 Lady Paladin Invitational and graduating to play on the Australian, European and Asian professional tours for four years from 1992-96.

Kelly loved the game of golf, but the brutal facts showed her a better career. She was good, but not quite good enough to compete on the U.S. Ladies Professional Golf Association's tour, the LPGA. However, Kelly has a great presence, excellent voice, and communication skills along with a tremendous knowledge of the game of golf. When Kelly combined the brutal facts with her passion for the game, she opened herself up to other means to find success.

Kelly became a fixture on The Golf Channel, the premier TV station for golf. Regarded as the station's most versatile on-air personality, she went on to host or co-anchor many of the station's programs. Kelly loves her work. She combined her passion for the game of golf and her communication skills to achieve success. Her passion for broadcasting so outweighs the idea of playing professional golf that Kelly cannot imagine doing anything else at this point in her career. Kelly loves her work—work she is passionate about and which allows her to take advantage of her skills.

Kelly's career and my hobby of playing rather than singing for my musical expression exemplify confronting the brutal facts. Combining passion and skills leads to a successful strategy. Consider the person who is passionate about fast cars. The glamour career is that of a racecar driver. Nevertheless, there are numerous means to finding happiness in the passion of fast cars: designer, mechanic, pit crewmember, owner, promoter, advertising, personal assistant, track developer, circuit administration, etc. The person with great reflexes and courage to face the danger of death should consider being the racecar driver, while the person who loves to solve problems, thinks outside the box, and likes to build things should consider the careers of designer, owner, or track developer. In order to build a successful strategy, we need to know our skills in addition to understanding and discovering our passion.

Passion + Skills = Strategy

Our Guiding Light

In *Good to Great,* Collins's second observation of disciplined thought for great companies summarizes the purpose of a successful strategy: "...they developed a simple, yet deeply insightful, frame of reference for all decisions."[73] A strategy should be a simple guiding light that you employ to fulfill your purpose. For example, in battle, a general's purpose is to win the battle; his strategy could be to divide and conquer. *How* he divides the enemy in order to conquer them is tactics. Another military strategy well practiced in numerous sectors of our society is that of pitting strength against weakness. We hear this weekly during football season as analysts discuss how one team will take advantage of their opponent's weakness. Attack the opponent's weakest point with your strength. Identifying the particular weaknesses and strengths are tactics. Consider these well-known strategies:

- Divide and conquer
- Attack weakness with strength

- Attack when the enemy least expects it
- Secrets should not be shared
- Take the path of least resistance

There are no details in these strategies. Strategy is not about the details; tactics are the details—the specifics about how to carry out a strategy. Walt Disney chose to fulfill his purpose to make people happy by creating wonderful movies and theme parks. What movies, what characters, what plots, what rides, etc., are the details—the tactics Walt had to decide on to execute his strategy. Red Skelton chose to fulfill his purpose to make people happy by being a comedian. What skits, what jokes, what costumes, etc., were the details—the tactics Red had to decide how to execute for his strategy of being a comedian. Strategies are not complex. To be the definitive guideline in all decision making, a strategy needs to be simple.

In *Good to Great,* Jim Collins provides the hedgehog concept to illustrate how great companies must clearly define simple strategies that everyone can understand and use as a beacon for making decisions. His hedgehog concept is based on Isaiah Berlin's famous essay *The Hedgehog and the Fox.* The central theme is based on an ancient parable: "The fox knows many things, but the hedgehog knows one big thing."[74] The fox, smart and cunning, creates many strategies to trap the hedgehog. All fail because the hedgehog has a simple strategy that makes the fox's crafty and sneaky plans fail every time. The hedgehog, a smaller version of the porcupine with sharp bristles on its back, simply curls up whenever the fox tries to attack. The fox spends countless hours trying to figure out how to capture the hedgehog. The hedgehog, on the other hand, does not concern itself with the fox; it goes about its day finding food and taking care of its offspring and its den. This essay divides people into two categories: foxes and hedgehogs. Foxes are smart and cunning. While able to focus on many things, they do not consolidate their thinking into a unified simple strategy. Hedgehogs, on the other hand, understand a simple yet powerful idea that guides, unifies and simplifies their world.

Strategies need to be like hedgehogs: simple and understandable so that they are easily seen and followed. Strategies are our guiding light. We should always consider whether what we are doing aligns with our strategy. If not, then we need to consider why we are doing it and how we can replace it with something that does adhere to our strategy.

* * *

From the dying, we know that our life purpose is to learn about and practice love. From a life perspective, a life strategy of creating positive feelings in ourselves and others not only allows us to work towards our life purpose, but it also heightens and optimizes our decision-making, problem solving, creative, and intuitive skills that optimizes our chances of creating success in all areas of our lives.

Applying the Principle of Strategy

From the principle of purpose, we learned the importance of correctly clarifying *what* it is we are doing, whether it is from a life perspective or from a professional or personal perspective. Anything we do—whether it is large or small—we should first clarify and understand *what* we are trying to accomplish.

The principle of strategy teaches us the next step—in any action we take—is figuring out *how* we plan to accomplish our objective. *What* did Walt Disney want to do? He wanted to make people happy. *How* did he go about achieving it? He created cartoons and movies. *What* did Mary Kay want to do? She wanted to give unlimited opportunity to women. *How* did she go about achieving it? She created a cosmetic company.

Looking back on a life such as Walt Disney's or Mary Kay's it may sometimes be hard to determine which came first: the *what* or the *how*. However, at some point the importance and dependency these two critical factors play in success is clear. In anything you do, first make sure you clearly understand *what* you are really trying to do and then figure out *how* you are going to do it before you actually start doing it. This is common sense, right? Then why is it so often ignored?

The programmer mentioned earlier did not take the time to understand fully *what* his manager wanted in a management tool. The lack of not understanding *what* he was supposed to build resulted in him having to rebuild the tool, taking an additional four weeks of work. Four weeks wasted because he did not take the time to understand *what*.

Our fast-paced modern society presses us to show progress. If we are not doing something then we are wasting time. To see someone sitting at a desk with their feet up on the desk, hands clasped behind their neck, just thinking, is not an acceptable portrait of productivity. We reward effort because it is easily visible. Effectiveness, doing it right the first time, is much harder to recognize because it seems so simple and easy. It's not! It appears easy because someone figured out how to make something complex, simple.

Effectiveness happens because someone took the time to put their feet up and figure out *how* to do it right the first time. When you figure it out as you go, it usually means redoing it. When you figure out *how* to do something before you do it, you continue to master the art of doing less and accomplishing more.

* * *

Principle Summary

Successful Living ABCs: Our *attitude* determines the *behavior* that causes the *consequences*.

> **Attitudes** *of love, caring, and compassion result in the* **Behavior** *that causes the* **Consequences** *that lead to joyful living.*

LIFE PRINCIPLES:

Purpose: To learn about and practice love.

Strategy: Create positive feelings in ourselves and others.

* * *

The following worksheets help identify a strategy for either a career or a personal strategy such as the one John Gray took with his wife. They help identify what you are passionate about and what your skills are to assist in creating a strategy to use as a guiding light for your future. You may be able to create a successfully strategy in one sitting. On the other hand, you may find it is something at which you will need to work, spending time contemplating, meditating or praying about before you clearly see your passions and skills and how they can perfectly blend into a simple guiding strategy.

While worksheets A and B address professional or personal strategies from a macro perspective, worksheet C provides space to apply the lesson of strategy—the *how*—to your everyday tasks, actions, or projects.

Principle 2 – Strategy

Worksheet A

Identifying Your Passions: Defining a strategy begins in identifying your interests.

Section 1: Answer these questions to jump-start your memory.

What do you spend your free time doing?

_____

_____

_____

_____

_____

What do you dream about doing and what do you want to change in your life?

_____

_____

_____

_____

What do you read about or study?

_____

_____

_____

_____

Section 2: Describe things about which you are passionate or have strong interests. These may or may not be the same items you listed in Section 1 of this worksheet and may be personal or professional:

_____

_____

_____

_____

Principle 2 – Strategy

Worksheet B

Identifying Your Talents: Step 2 in identifying a strategy is to take an inventory of your strengths and talents.

Strengths and Talents: Describe what you believe your strengths and talents are:

_____

_____

_____

_____

_____

Principle 2 – Strategy

Worksheet C

Creating a Strategy: Write a professional or personal strategy.

Purpose: Copy your personal or career purpose from your Principle 1 Worksheet:

_____

_____

_____

_____

_____

Strategy: Describe your professional or personal strategy.

_____

_____

_____

_____

_____

How: Select a project or activity and clearly describe how you intend to accomplish the objective.

_____

_____

_____

_____

_____

PART 2: ENTRAINMENT GUIDELINES

Section 3 - Leadership

"Big things of the world
Can only be achieved by attending to their small begin-
nings."

Lao Tzu[75]

Part 2 of this book addresses guidelines we can use to help focus on and create positive feelings in our lives. It provides a foundation upon which to build heart / brain entrainment while creating habits that naturally mature our emotional intelligence.

This first section of Part 2 reveals our third key principle to creating a successful life: leadership.

Leadership: A Story

Sanjeev felt the hot sun as it bore down upon him and his soldiers. Sanjeev, a newly promoted Captain in His Highness's army, sat astride his horse with a straight back and head held high as if he could touch the sun if he so desired. This was how His Highness rode and so it would be how Sanjeev would ride. He was proud of his new position as head of tax collections for His Highness. As Captain, he would determine what each subject would pay. When he asked for money, part of their crops or their animals in payment of their taxes, he knew he could take what he wanted. He now had power over them and he would enjoy it. They feared His Highness and thus they would continue to fear him. Riding on his horse, the sun brought forth sweat upon his brow, neck, and back; and his desire brought forth the idea into his mind.

He told the people His Highness had doubled their taxes—although His Highness had ordered no such thing. They cried and begged him to help. They could not live if His Highness took so much. Therefore, Sanjeev demonstrated pity towards them. He gave them back one-fourth of what he had taken, telling them he would watch over them and protect them from their greedy ruler—a ruler so powerful he required his subjects to get on their hands and knees and prostrate themselves before him whenever they found themselves in his presence. The people thanked Sanjeev and kissed his hand. Sanjeev received their kisses and dreamed of the day when they would prostrate themselves before him. Sanjeev gave twenty-five percent of what he took back to the people. He gave fifty percent to His Highness, twenty percent he kept for himself, and the remaining five percent he again gave to His Highness, who rewarded him for his effectiveness in collecting what belonged to His Highness.

Sanjeev's plan worked. The subjects begged the soldiers to support Sanjeev, as he would make a better king, for he cared for them and His Highness did not. It was His Highness, not Sanjeev, who had doubled their taxes and was starving them. In time, Sanjeev easily overthrew His Highness. He placed the dead body on a pole outside the castle to show the people His Highness no longer controlled them. The people rejoiced. If they would obey Sanjeev, he would make this land the greatest of all lands.

However, the people did not find relief from Sanjeev, who now wore the crown and title of His Highness. Sanjeev's taste of being king satisfied neither his appetite for power nor his hunger for control. He sent his armies beyond his borders and conquered his neighbors and his neighbors' neighbors. Forced to mine metal for weapons, forge the metal into weapons, or work the fields to supply his armies with food, Sanjeev's subjects grew weaker, angry and full of hate while the soil grew barren. Sanjeev rode his horse among his subjects, held his head high and felt the sun beat upon his face. He no longer noticed the subjects prostrating themselves before him, their face kissing the dirt upon which he trod as he sat astride his beautiful black horse. The people longed for

His Highness, whose skeleton still hung on the pole outside Sanjeev's castle.

One day, Maktub, one of the most skilled weapon makers, received a block of ore. Maktub learned his brother's life had been lost in the mining of this block of ore. As a young boy, Maktub helped his father cast metals, shape horseshoes and create swords and axes. His father placed food upon the family table by trading his skills as a blacksmith for payment from the local people and His Highness, the one who now hung from the pole outside Sanjeev's castle. Maktub learned the art of shaping metal from his father, but he watched in awe as the sun drew the crops forth from the earth while the heavens watered them. Maktub's father let him and his brother plant a small crop each year. He did this to satisfy Maktub's yearning to be near the earth, not because of need. Maktub loved the feel of freshly plowed dirt under his feet. He and his brother would remove their shoes and walk in it. The softness of the dirt covered their feet as its coolness refreshed their souls. Maktub felt at home when working the small crops. It was the memory of his crops and dirt between his toes Maktub would recall as he shaped metal for Sanjeev's armies. Maktub's heart ached for the silence of crops growing. Instead, his ears were full of men's hammers as they created more weapons, and the silence of the land contained little growth.

Maktub would dream at night of a land overflowing with growth, crops yielding nourishment for the people and the people freely giving their energy to the crops. Maktub told his companions, his friends and the other shapers of metal about his dreams and swore to them it would one day be true. Maktub, the shaper of metal, remained at heart Maktub, the farmer—for Maktub's dreams planted the seeds of hope within those around him. Wherever Maktub went, people followed and began to ask, "How can we make this happen, Maktub?" Maktub did not know. He only knew more and more people asked him with each passing day.

The day the block of ore, which his brother's life was lost in its mining, came to Maktub he began the process of transforming the ore into a weapon for Sanjeev's army. With an aching heart, tears flowed from his face and evaporated as they landed in the liquid metal. He made the greatest sword he had ever made and he swore Sanjeev would never have it. He would hide it if necessary because the sword contained the soul of his brother and the spirit of Maktub—these things Sanjeev could not have.

When Maktub finished the sword, men stood in awe of his creation. Stories of the sword's creation slid easily throughout the land and thrust Maktub's dreams of a prosperous land into the soul of the people—for Maktub had carved his dream on the sword's blade and the stories of the sword plunged the dream into the people's hearts.

The General of Sanjeev's armies summoned Maktub to the castle wanting to know of the sword with the dream written on its blade. The General ordered Maktub to fetch the sword and come back, this time to see Sanjeev. Escorted by guards, Maktub returned with the sword and started to kneel to prostrate himself in front of Sanjeev. The General seized his arm before he could kneel and brought him back to his feet. This angered Sanjeev, but the General began to speak. The General told Sanjeev that Maktub had stirred the people, causing them to believe Maktub would be a better king than Sanjeev; after all, Maktub's way adorned the blade of a powerful sword. Sanjeev ordered the General to kill Maktub with the very weapon created by Maktub. The General bowed to Sanjeev. He promised Sanjeev that Maktub would never again make a sword. He then motioned to his guards to seize Sanjeev. Sanjeev struggled but to no avail. The soldiers first followed the General and then whomever the General followed. The General moved in front of Sanjeev and said, "The soldiers obey you, Sanjeev, but they follow me. The people obey you also, Sanjeev, but they follow Maktub. From now on, I will follow Maktub as will the people." He then ordered the Guards to place Sanjeev on the pole outside of Maktub's castle.

Centuries would pass and people would tell stories of Maktub and how, in the spring, he would go to his people's crops, remove his shoes, and walk barefoot in the freshly plowed fields. The land and people prospered greatly; they lived in a blessed land protected by a powerful sword and the heart of a great leader. Stories of Maktub passed down from generation to generation until Maktub, his kingdom and the sword became a legend. Like all legends, facts and myth merge until time can no longer tell which is which. As for Maktub, his land became known as Camelot, and its King pulled a great sword, Excalibur, from a stone. But the truth was that Maktub only followed his heart, and the people followed Maktub.

Walking Our Path

It is easy to follow what those before us have done. I know, for as Sanjeev followed the ways of His Highness, I too followed the ways of corporate America. I behaved as many of us behave. I behaved according to how I thought others wanted me to behave. I spent an entire career being a workalcoholic, struggling with corporate America, not balancing work and family, missing the enjoyment of today, worrying about tomorrow and fretting over the past—years wasted on the pursuit of the American dream. A lifetime behavior pattern of worrying and trying to control the future did not bring the happiness or abundance I sought.

Yet our behavior is critical to success. Our behavior reflects our attitude. Part 1 of this book revealed the right attitude. If *attitudes of love, caring, and compassion* result in the *behavior* that causes the *consequences* that lead to joyful living, what then is the right behavior? To understand the right behavior, and why that behavior pattern is critical to success, we will explore:

- what the prophets of history tell us the right behavior is,

- what our parents and the dying say the right behavior is, and

- what, when we listen, corporate America tells us is the right behavior.

The behavior pattern extolled by the prophets of history, taught by our parents, expressed by the dying, and even demonstrated by business, tells us the right behavior for successful living. Our behavior should be one that optimizes our chances of success. Hence, we examine why our selected behavior pattern works and how we make it work. We look at:

- what happens when we practice the right behavior, and

- review what science says we need to do to make it work.

Entrainment is central to our understanding of the right attitudes of caring and compassion. Caring and compassion create positive emotions that in turn create entrainment, which places us in optimal creative, intuitive and problem solving states. Entrainment is also central in our understanding of the right behavior. This section concludes by examining:

- the four types of behavior patterns and how they encourage or discourage entrainment, and

- real world examples of applying our behavior strategy to our everyday problems.

What the Prophets Say

Treat others as you would like to be treated; this is the essence of the wisdom of Christ, the prophet of Christianity—the religion I learned as a black-haired, blue-eyed innocent boy of five. Christ is only one of many who speak this message. 500 years before Christ, Gautama Buddha uttered the words: *Consider others as yourself* (Dhammapada 10.1).[76] Lao Tsu's message that a violent man will die a violent death echoes a similar philosophy. Mohammad, Mother Teresa, Gandhi and a host of other prophets all speak the same simple message. Stripping away religion and doctrine, we find a simple teaching from the prophets of history: *treat others the way you would like to be treated.*

Is it possible this simple message could be one of the secrets for success? On the surface it certainly does not appear to be a strategy that brings abundance and happiness. I ignored applying this message as an approach for finding abundance for many years. Houses, cars, family and making it all turn out a certain way seemed the logical areas on which to focus. After all, we traditionally define success by those areas. While the wisdom of the great prophets made sense to me from a religious and moral perspective, it did not make sense as a behavior strategy for everyday abundance. I was not sitting in a cave meditating, isolated from the troubles of the world. I was in the middle of the real world, with real issues, where nice guys finish last. As for me, I did not have the time to listen to a strategy that did not logically appear to translate to success.

Therefore, I ignored it. Not that I was not a nice guy; most people who knew me during that time would say I was a nice guy. I simply did not make *treat others the way you would like to be treated* my primary focus. However, the patients at hospice facing their own death convinced me to try another approach. I slowly started to hear their message: life is about caring, caring about the people with whom you live *and* the people with whom you work. How you behave towards them reflects and expresses that caring. How you treat others simply defines who you are. From this perspective, how we treat each other did make sense. However, from a corporate perspective, I could not find the courage to apply this philosophy for finding prosperity and climbing the corporate ladder.

It is no surprise the great prophets and founders of religion teach a simple, easy and straightforward message about behavior. We find at the center of their message an attitude of love and a behavior of treating each other the ways we would like to be treated. Watching the dying convinced me it was more important than my corporate objectives and gave me the courage to apply the lesson I was hearing. In doing so, I changed my life.

What the Dying and Our Parents Say

Early in my management career, my company sent me to a management training class where I learned a manager spends one day a week (one-fifth of his or her time) correcting miscommunications within the organization. At the time, I found this hard to believe, but with many additional years of management experience under my belt I now know it to be true. In that class, I learned ways and methods to help facilitate effective communication. However, it is not what we say or how we say it, how we organize it or in what media we choose to present it that helps correct the majority of miscommunications. It is not what we do that helps the most, it is what we usually do not do that makes the biggest impact—instead of talking, I learned how to listen.

I listen more now than ever before. At hospice, I listen when I am making someone's bed. I listen when I am feeding someone. I listen when I help give a bath. What I hear is much of what Dr. Elisabeth Kübler-Ross learned:

> "The dying learn a great deal at the end of life, usually when it is too late to apply."[77]

The dying say caring, compassion and love are the most important things in our lives and they tell me their regrets. Frances regretted not learning to fly when given a rare opportunity not usually granted to women in the first half of the 20th century. Ada was different. She learned to fly a crop-dusting biplane. She wasn't given an opportunity to be taught; rather, she and her brother learned by the seat of their pants, taking off and landing in the fields by the family barn. For each potential adventure not taken advantage of, there is a story of adventure that should be a movie.

The real regrets, the ones that tug at the heart and soul of the dying are the ones about how they behaved (or maybe I should say misbehaved) towards someone … a brother, a sister, a mother, a best friend, etc. When the dying take their last breath, these are the regrets they take with them. These regrets reveal the secrets of the dying: "If only I had treated them better."

* * *

While the dying tell me about their loved ones and the importance of how we treat them, it is our parents, our brothers and sisters who first teach us about caring and how we should treat each other. Our parents teach us as children to respect our elders, to love one another, and to be honest. As children, our parents, aunts, uncles, brothers and sisters all tell us how to behave. When we listen to our parents, they repeat the same message as the prophets—treat others with respect, honesty, honor, trust, value, care and kindness.

As we grow up, we begin to experience these lessons. We experience what happens when we do not treat others the way we would like to be treated. In the eyes of being a teenager, of puppy love and infatuation, our heart awakens to the longing of finding our "one true love in life." However, we are not alone in this path. Our parents, uncles, aunts, their parents and their parents' parents back to the beginning of human-kind have all sought out and experienced the feeling of being in love, of finding the one person with whom to spend the rest of our lives. We search for something our scientists can never prove, touch or measure; yet we all know of its existence, and we all have done sheer stupidity in its name. Once we find that person, our normal behavior transforms us into characters our friends sometimes do not recognize. We bring flowers, we write love poems; if our parents knew we did these things, it would make them proud. It is in these infatuations we learn what happens when we don't treat our one true love as we would like to be treated. Eventually a lie is told, a commitment is missed and we lose the one that meant so much to us. When we step back and pay attention, when we really listen, our life experiences teach us the same lessons our parents taught us as children: treat others as we would like to be treated.

* * *

Walking through the doors of corporate America and adult-hood, we act and behave in a different way. We begin to focus on cars, houses, money and all the other things on which life demands we focus. Here the rules are different. In a dog-eat-dog world, people must learn to look out for themselves and our "treat others as ourselves" attitude becomes viewed as a hindrance.

Not knowing whether to believe my parents and the dying or believe my corporate peers on how to get ahead, I did what most engineers or scientists do—I did an experiment. I took the simple philosophy of *treat people the way you would like to be treated* and began to apply it at work. I really did be-

155

lieve this would be the end of my climbing the corporate ladder. That is not how you get to the top, but I was willing to take the chance and try. The message was too loud and coming from too many voices for me to ignore, and that is when my life turned around. One thing after another started to fall into place. Good luck, synchronicity, coincidence; whatever it was, I did not want it to go away. Later, I would stumble onto the scientific reasons of how entrainment works.

It was actually very simple. When I treated others the way I wanted to be treated, I felt good about myself. Those around me felt good about how I treated them. The positive feelings created were placing us in states of entrainment and enhancing our problem solving, creativity and intuitive abilities. I, by my behavior pattern of treating others how I wished to be treated, was creating entrainment and tilting the odds of success in my favor. It explained why things seemed to be falling into place with less effort, why things were more synchronous, and why I was accomplishing more with seemingly less effort. I had stumbled onto something and for the first time in my life, I was experiencing joyful living. I realized both the inside and the outside worlds were gently repeating a continuous message. The same message repeated from generation to generation, love one another and treat others the way you would want to be treated.

What Business Says

Our basic need to love and be loved is also accompanied by other basic needs, among them the desire to be respected and trusted. David H. Maister, a world leader on the subject of the management of professional companies, says in his book, *Practice What you Preach—What Managers Must Do to Create a High Achievement Culture*, that trust and respect are factors that weigh heavily in profitability.[78] Maister surveyed 139 offices in 29 firms, in 15 countries, in 15 different lines of business on the topic of whether employee attitudes correlated to financial success. He surprisingly found that *attitudes* were what drove financial results. [79] Success was not so much about policies, he discovered, but about personalities practicing what they preached: trust, respect and integrity.

What behavior results in trust, respect and integrity? The answer: treat others the way you would like to be treated. When we do, others perceive us as trustworthy. People believe you will treat them fairly. After all, it is how you would want others to treat you, is it not? Integrity naturally follows and respect thereafter. Maister indicates that successful managers of superstar companies have figured out that building your people is a fundamental priority. It starts by actually *caring* about and having a *real concern* for the employees. That means showing a real interest in what happens in their lives, who they are and what they need and want. Maister's studies show that managers in superstar companies have learned that success is about respect, character, integrity, honesty, trust, empowerment, loyalty, confidence and keeping promises.[80] Maister's conclusion is very similar to the words echoed by the dying; success in business is more about relationships than it is about the work.[81]

Management is about relationships, work is about relationships and life is about relationships. The above findings from Maister's research show that who we are, and how we treat each other, are critical to success. Who we are is our *attitude* and how we treat each other is our *behavior*.

If attitude is fundamental to success, we need a behavior pattern that reinforces the right attitudes. Our behavior must reflect our attitude; our behavior needs to build trust, respect, integrity, honesty, empowerment, confidence and loyalty—the same characteristics David Maister identifies as fundamental to building high achieving organizations. We need a behavior pattern that treats others the way we would like to be treated.

The Results of the Right Behavior

What happens when we treat others the way we would like to be treated? First, we feel good about ourselves. Second, others feel good about how we treated them. Those positive emotions, according to our scientists, create heart / brain entrainment within oneself and within others. Entrainment enhances the awareness of problems and their solutions, heightens our intuition and increases synchronicity allowing better problem solving ability, greater perception of opportunities, and creativity.

Scientifically, treating others the way we would like to be treated, places us in the optimal state to achieve success. It explains one critical element in why superstar companies are so successful: they value an attitude of caring and build a culture around a behavior pattern that reinforces the right attitude.

This behavior strategy—to treat others as we would like to be treated—builds trust, respect, integrity, honesty, empowerment, confidence and loyalty—those same characteristics of high achieving businesses. Our behavior pattern produces the very characteristics Maister claims are mandatory for success. Maister's research on what makes companies successful reveals a culture that inherently promotes entrainment.

Our behavior guideline is now clear: treat others the way we would like to be treated. In chapter 3, we established the proper attitude:

> *Attitudes* of love, caring, and compassion determine the *behavior* that causes the consequences that lead to success.

Attitudes of love, caring, and compassion naturally lead to a behavior of treating others the way we would want to be treated. Thus, the right behavior reflects the right attitude.

> *Attitudes* of love, caring, and compassion result in the *behavior* of treating others the way you want to be treated, that causes the *consequences* that lead to success.

Science Shows Us How to Make It Work

Our management ABCs teach us that attitude determines behavior. B.F. Skinner, and his introduction of behaviorism as a science in the 1950s, shows behavior can and does shape our attitudes. A simple strategy of treating others as we wish to be treated can and does develop attitudes of caring and compassion, the emotions needed for entrainment.

Skinner points out children who grow up in a Christian-based society generally become Christian, while children who grow up in a Moslem-based society generally grow up to become Moslem.[82] Hence, outside factors influence our attitudes and beliefs; they are not solely determined from our inner being. We can use outside factors to help mold and shape them:

> To change attitude, reward the behavior that reflects the desired attitude.

At the core of Skinner's behaviorism is the concept of conditioning. Providing a pigeon with food each time it raises its head above a certain level will lead to the pigeon raising its head when it wants food. Skinner also reveals emotional responses in humans can be conditioned and this explains why emotional intelligence is not fixed like IQ. If emotional responses can be conditioned, and our emotional response is at the core of emotional intelligence, then emotional intelligence can be modified.

At a base level, our need to survive has top priority. Once we can survive, we respond to stimuli that address our feelings. Skinner uses the example that we like delicious food. Thus, we can be conditioned to like the stimuli associated with delicious food. A salesperson buys his client dinner. This creates an association between the pleasure of eating and the salesperson. Skinner reports people can grow to like a certain type of music if they listen to it while they eat.[83]

Behavioral conditioning is at the core of creating behavior patterns reflecting either the right attitude for success or the wrong attitude. Corporate America, for example, has a long history of rewarding the wrong behavior. We preach work smart, but we reward the hard worker. Consider this example:

> Two managers give their assistants a 500-page document whose matching data files are lost. In addition to a clean copy, each manager has also marked up a second copy with a number of changes in red ink. The changes include paragraphs moved and sentences rewritten, with notes trailing sideways in the margins, and others going across and onto the back of the page. One assistant spends the next week furiously typing to get the manuscript retyped into the computer. The assistant works the weekend in order to have the document on the boss's desk by the following Monday morning. The manager recognizes the effort put forth by the assistant and makes the assistant the employee of the month and a lit-

tle something extra shows up in the next paycheck as a one-time bonus for saving the boss's neck.

Our other assistant takes a different approach. After looking at the assignment, the assistant spends the next two hours talking to a number of people. The boss notices this and becomes a little frustrated. *Doesn't the assistant know how important this is?* In those two hours, the assistant discovers who in the building has a scanner and the associated Optical Character Recognition software to scan in the document and convert it into a word processing format. After lunch, the assistant scans in the 500 pages, makes the necessary changes, and by 4:00 places the finished document on the boss's desk. The assistant then asks if the boss does not have anything urgent for her, could she leave a little early as there is a soccer game to which she would love to take her 13 year-old son. As the assistant walks out of the building, she passes the other assistant who has already re-typed 38 pages into the computer—the beginning of becoming employee of the month along with a nice little bonus for her hard work. The boss watches the assistant leave. With the completed document in hand and not one error in the whole manuscript, the boss thinks, Slacker.

Do not do this. Do not reward hard work. Appreciate hard work, thank your employees when hard work is required, but never reward it. Reward the smart work. The boss in the above example should have paid for the soccer tickets. While one assistant sacrifices their week and weekend, the other will have the rest of the week to do other productive tasks for her manager because she found a better, cheaper, quicker way to do a job. Reward the work smart attitude and behavior. A manager who rewards smart work and an assistant who works smart is going to get more work done in a shorter time than a manager who rewards hard work and an assistant who works hard but does not take the time to think and relate.

* * *

Working smart is a much better way to be successful than working hard. However, it was only after I found the courage to put how I treated others as my top priority that I began to learn the true meaning of working smart—doing less and accomplishing more. Somehow, I noticed success was happening more often and with less effort on my part the more I paid attention to treating others the way I wanted to be treated.

Positive emotions create entrainment. A simple method to create positive emotions is to treat others the way you would like to be treated. As a manager, reward behavior that reflects this attitude. The basic need for approval, attention and affection that we all seek will eventually mold the behavior of your employees, your peers or your supervisors. Modifying behavior occurs based on the rewards or reinforcements provided. Make sure you reward the right behavior and slowly, one by one, those around you will develop the right attitudes. Just as children who are reared in a Christian society generally grow up to be Christians, and children who are reared in a Moslem society generally grow up to be Moslems, so will employees reared in an environment that rewards the concept of *considering others as yourself* grow up to consider others as themselves. The entrainment that results places you and others in the best position to succeed in whatever you undertake.

A favorite passages from David H. Maister's book on creating a high achieving culture is from an incident documented by Lisa Endlich who relates the story of an eager young employee who at every opportunity, using one technique or another, let their manager know that "I did this!" One day, the manager casually mentioned that at that company they say "We, not I" and then moved on.[84]

Not only does this illustrate how teamwork belongs ahead of individual performance, but the heart of this story is the concept that everyone contributes, everyone is part of the team and everyone gets the recognition and rewards of success.

In order to develop attitudes of caring and compassion, employ a simple behavior pattern of treating others the way you wish to be treated. It does not change things overnight, but inch-by-inch the world around us changes, we change and the people around us change. This is what leaders do—they change the world. Reward yourself and reward others when they behave in a manner that reinforces the right attitudes. Here are my top three behaviors I like to reward at work:

- Working Smart—do not fall into the trap of rewarding hard work. Whenever you see someone find a better way, reward it. You will be surprised how quickly this attitude spreads when reinforced by management. I know; my employees constantly bring up the fact a particular way is not the smart thing to do. It only took six months to modify one organization from being proud of being the hardest workers in town to being an organization looking for the smart solution. There will always be periods of working hard, but it should be the last option rather than the first.

- Teamwork—Reward the people who say, "We did it." People who say, "I did it," tend to be Rulers and Slaves. People who say, "We did it," tend to be Leaders and Followers. Reward the behavior that will help teach Rulers and Slaves to be Leaders and Followers.

- Values—Stress the values you want to create, in particular, treating others the way you want to be treated. Some of the objectives I put into every employee's goals for the coming year are: teamwork, work smart, makes others more valuable, balances work and home and treats others the way they would like to be treated. I let employees know these items will be part of their upcoming performance review and salary increase.

Reward behavior that creates the attitudes you seek, in oneself and in those around you. Skinner's concept of behaviorism indicates those attitudes will begin to form within the individual, group, and in oneself if you reward the desired behavior. Success will not be far behind.

The Entrainment Quadrants

The Entrainment Quadrants, as shown below, represent four categories into which people may be classified. Of the four quadrants, some foster heart / brain entrainment while others discourage it.

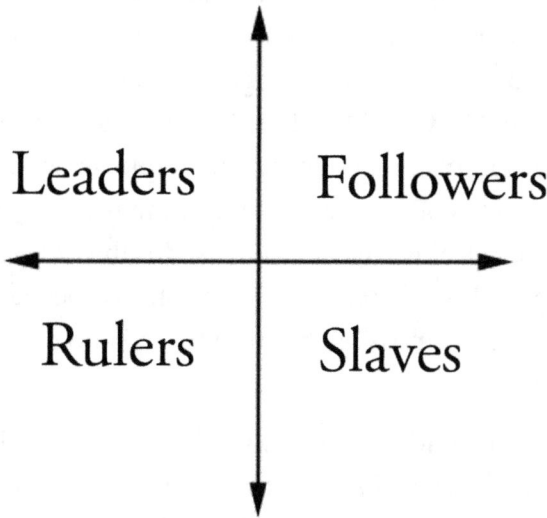

Leaders	Followers
Rulers	Slaves

Rulers:

A ruler needs a kingdom. Obtaining and maintaining a kingdom dominates a ruler's goals and objectives. A ruler gives priority to the kingdom or their quest for a kingdom over the people. Look at the resulting attitudes:

- Obtaining a kingdom often gives rise to attitudes of greed, ambition, manipulation, exploitation and sabotage.

- Maintaining a kingdom often promotes attitudes of control, power, dominance and fear (of losing one's kingdom).

- Enjoying one's kingdom attracts attitudes of superiority, self-indulgence, authority, decadence and righteousness.

Men such as Napoleon, Stalin, Hitler, and our own story's character, Sanjeev, are classic examples of great rulers of great kingdoms. However, kingdoms can also be small, almost invisible. Consider the father who dominates the family, the controlling child, or the employee who carves out and protects his or her small piece of the world by not allowing anyone else to learn how to do the job. While the employee builds job security, he or she is locked in a cage. Promotion is not possible because there is no one to take his or her place.

On the other hand, having a kingdom does not classify you as a ruler. Abraham Lincoln ruled during the most perilous of times in the history of the United States, yet one labels Lincoln not as a ruler, but as a leader of men.

Slaves:

Images of slaves being whipped as they moved blocks of stone to build pyramids, or people living in poverty conditions as they picked cotton to support the lavish lifestyles of their plantation owners, come to mind when we think of slaves. Slaves come in many forms: the subjects of Sanjeev in our story, prisoners of war, an abused and dominated spouse or a divorced secretary struggling to support her children by working for a domineering boss because she has no visible alternatives. Some slaves can easily identify the source of their enslavement while others can be unaware of their enslavement. Mistreated, slaves harbor feelings of anger and hatred; rebellions, anarchy and mutinies can follow. Hatred, anger and violence, along with feelings of fear, sadness, sorrow, dread and apprehension are all possible characteristics of slaves.

While Sanjeev is a ruler, he is also part slave. Until he overthrew His Highness, he was the subject to His Highness and this caused him to plan and execute his escape from and overthrow of His Highness. Once established as the ruler, he became enslaved to: 1) his kingdom, 2) his hunger for power and control and 3) his fear of losing his kingdom. Fear, sadness, sorrow, dread, and apprehension, along with dormant feelings of hatred, anger and violence are all possible characteristics of slaves.

Slaves can be excellent workers, managers or owners, yet carry the slave attitude that they are victims and hold anger in their hearts towards their company, managers, workers or co-workers.

* * *

Summarizing and plotting the attitudes of Rulers and Slaves on our Entrainment Quadrants shows a pattern of negative feelings—those characteristics known to discourage and decrease heart / brain entrainment. Instead of increasing our problem-solving abilities, our intuitive abilities, and our synchronicity, the emotions resulting from the attitudes of Rulers and Slaves do the opposite—they decrease our physical, mental, spiritual and emotional effectiveness.

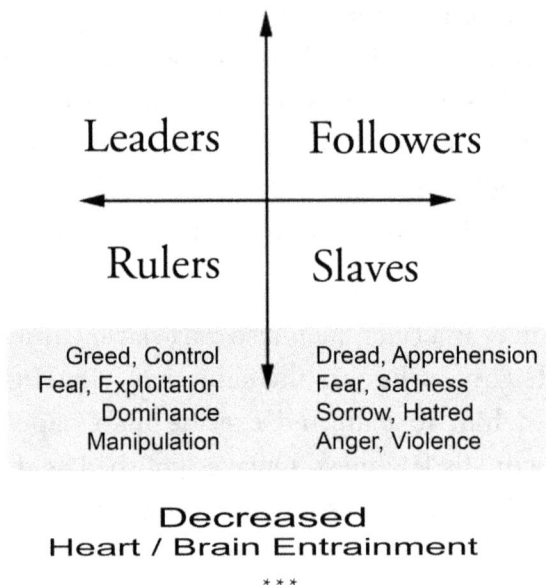

Leaders	Followers
Rulers	Slaves
Greed, Control Fear, Exploitation Dominance Manipulation	Dread, Apprehension Fear, Sadness Sorrow, Hatred Anger, Violence

**Decreased
Heart / Brain Entrainment**

* * *

Leaders:

Leaders are easily recognized—people follow them. They follow because they want to, not because they are told to or forced to. Leaders rise from among the people as naturally as a plant reaches towards the sun. Pulled towards something greater, others see that and follow. Their goal is not to build a kingdom to rule, but to create and accomplish something of which all are proud. They do not utter the words "I did it." They shout, "We did it!" The people also shout it and celebrate together their accomplishments.

Some leaders stand in front, some are vocal, some stand in the rear and remain silent—they lead by example. Leaders come in all shapes and sizes, hold all types of positions and lead in different ways, but they have common attributes. Most noticeable is their ability to care about a goal and all those involved in the pursuit of that goal. Truth, justice and the American way are the trademarks of the Superman comic strip character. He goes to extremes to see that not one individual is injured while fighting the bad guys. Gandhi's compassion led an entire nation and inspired countless numbers to follow his example. The peacefulness of the Buddha, the love of Jesus and the courage of Helen Keller has changed humankind.

The attributes of caring and compassion distinguish great leaders from rulers. While both possess passion—the fuel that drives them—leaders inherently reflect our life purpose; they demonstrate love and compassion. People naturally follow leaders, and why not? Attitudes and behaviors that reflect our life purpose should attract with ease and comfort. It only seems natural that rulers and anything else that goes against our life purpose would require force, effort, and struggle to find their idea of success. Following our life's purpose places us in the flow of positive energy. It creates positive feelings that optimize our body and mind to find success with less effort because we begin to exist within a harmonious relationship with the world and those around us.

Followers:

The attributes of Followers closely resemble the attributes of Leaders. We have already seen this similarity between Rulers and Slaves; a Slaves' resistance meets a Ruler's force. The negative emotions generated by the attributes of Rulers breed similar negative emotions within their Slaves. Conversely, Followers freely accept their Leaders' care and compassion. The positive emotions generated by the attributes of Leaders foster similar positive emotions within their followers.

Leaders care for and protect their Followers, and in turn, Followers freely choose to care for and protect their Leaders. Followers have a freedom that Slaves do not. Followers feel the same desire to create and reach the goal of the Leader because the Leader and the Followers share the same goals. The needs of the Leader do not outweigh the needs of the Followers or vice versa. Followers feel a part of something greater than themselves. They strive for the common good of all. They share the load and take on the work freely because they see that they and everyone benefits.

Without Followers the work is not done, the goal never achieved, the success never realized. Followers and Leaders form a team, each contributing in their own way to the success of the whole. Caring, compassion, freedom, sharing, connection, creating and belonging are all attributes of Followers.

* * *

Summarizing and plotting the attitudes of Leaders and Followers on our Entrainment Quadrants show a pattern of positive feelings, those characteristics known to create heart / brain entrainment. These positive feelings increase our problem-solving and creative abilities, our intuitive abilities and our synchronicity—the elements needed for joyful living.

Increased
Heart / Brain Entrainment

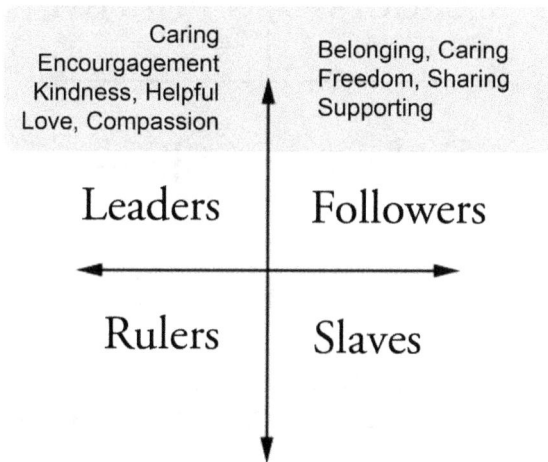

Caring Encourgagement Kindness, Helpful Love, Compassion	Belonging, Caring Freedom, Sharing Supporting
Leaders	**Followers**
Rulers	**Slaves**

In combining the attributes for all four Entrainment Quadrants, we easily see Rulers and Slaves behave in a way that creates negative emotions, which in turn discourages heart / brain entrainment. We also see Leaders and Followers behave in a way that creates positive emotions, which in turn induces heart / brain entrainment.

Increased
Heart / Brain Entrainment

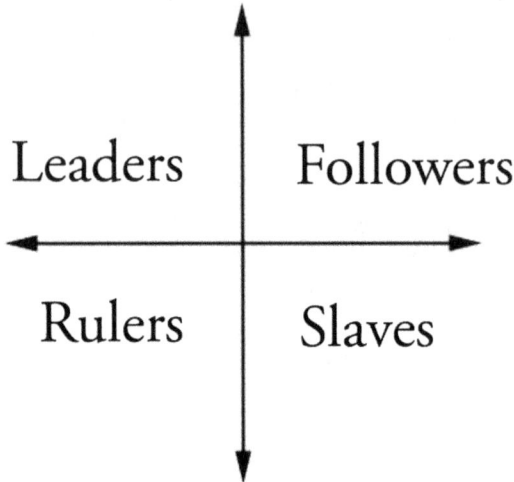

Leaders | Followers

Rulers | Slaves

Decreased
Heart / Brain Entrainment

Our challenge is to orient ourselves, or an organization, above the horizontal entrainment line separating Rulers and Slaves from Leaders and Followers. Thus, an organization oriented for success is one that: 1) hires Leaders and Followers, and 2) rewards behavior to help Rulers and Slaves transition into Leaders and Followers. This second aspect is also the key for individual success. If someone is a Ruler or Slave, it does not mean he or she cannot become a Leader or Follower. Our management ABCs teach it is our *attitude* that is the key to behavior and consequences. Fortunately, attitude is not fixed.

"He's a changed man," is the moral of many stories and it was the person's attitude that changed. Sometimes, it takes a personal tragedy before someone comes to his or her senses:

the death of someone close, cancer, divorce or a lost job. These events ask questions and cause awakenings; *attitudes* are changed and people learn what is important. The dying, our parents, business, or our knowledge about entrainment all stress the importance of behaving in a manner that demonstrates caring and love in our lives—a behavior pattern central to a successful life.

A Simple Guideline

I find the simple strategy of treating others the way you wish to be treated to be more than a philosophy or attitude you can apply in your life or work to bring about successful living. It is also a great aid in making difficult decisions.

In the management class where I learned about listening, we learned a simple technique to improve our listening ability: we practiced repeating back to the other person what we believe that person had said. Once we could express the other person's opinion in our own words, we then expressed our opinion. Placing ourselves in a position where we understood the other person's perspective allowed us to proceed with the understanding needed to facilitate effective communications.

The effectiveness of this simple listening technique is amazing. When people hear their own ideas and words repeated back to them, feelings of empathy, understanding and caring arise. It becomes OK for you to have a difference of opinion as they realize you do understand their concerns. Hearing one's own perspective from someone else creates the feeling of empathy. People are more likely to be cooperative in resolving differences when they really listen to the other person.

The effectiveness of good listening makes sense now that we know how entrainment works. The act of good listening creates positive feelings, placing both people involved in a state of entrainment. Seeing a situation from the other person's perspective is the key to effective listening and our behavior strategy of treating others how we would like to be treated.

In most situations, we are aware of how we would like to be treated. What is important is our ability to see how others would like to be treated.

* * *

Listening to our scientists and the new understanding of entrainment, to the great prophets of history, to the dying, to our parents, or the new studies of what makes companies successful, the message is clear: compassion, love and caring are the keys to success. These feelings create states of efficiency, better solutions and higher states of awareness because they create heart / brain entrainment within individuals and within organizations. A behavior pattern that reflects, builds and reinforces these attitudes will create an environment where success happens more naturally, with less effort and more ease.

Principle 3: Leadership

Our third key principle to successful living, leadership, goes beyond being a leader of men and women. It addresses personal leadership in taking responsibility for the leadership of one's own life. Whether we are a ruler, slave, follower or leader in our relationship to others, we are first, and foremost, the leader of our own life. Personal leadership echoes the same attributes as being a leader of others. Its application means taking responsibility and accountability for your own life rather than for a group of people.

Leadership, like purpose and strategy, can be difficult to discover. Once understood, its beauty and effectiveness lie in its simplicity. People follow leaders because leaders walk in a direction in which others also want to walk. Natural leaders know the direction in which they are walking (leadership), why they are going there (purpose) and how to get there (strategy). When corporate leaders fail to express a company's purpose and strategy, the company goes in many directions at once, somewhat like the fox in the story of the hedgehog. The company, management and workers are scattered. Without purpose, passion fades. Without passion, motivation disappears. Without motivation, movement halts. Without movement, progress does not occur. Without purpose and strategy, leadership cannot succeed at the corporate level.

However, when purpose and strategy are defined, leadership becomes the simple act of sharing that purpose and strategy, and ensuring it is executed. Whether it is Bill Gates or Robin Hood, having a purpose and strategy makes the act of leadership simple. Robin Hood accomplished his purpose to help the workers and farmers by executing a strategy of robbing the rich and giving to the poor. Robin's job as leader of his band of merry men was simple: make sure his men knew their purpose and execute the strategy of robbing the rich and giving to the poor.

Alignment with Life Purpose and Life Strategy:

Successful corporate leaders share the vision (purpose and strategy) and ensure its execution. However, one additional secret propels truly great companies. They have inherently, and maybe unknowingly, aligned their corporate purpose and culture with our life purpose and our life strategy.

Examine the purposes for those companies listed in section 2—Purpose. The great majority of these company purposes are in alignment with our life purpose to learn about and practice love. These companies want to "help make the world a better place to live." They want to "make people happy," "help women excel," "make contributions for the advancement of humanity," "be a role model for society," and "improve human life."

David H. Maister's criteria for the qualities needed for high achieving corporate cultures point out successful corporate cultures are in alignment with our life strategy to create positive feelings. They want people to feel good. They want to create environments that result in the qualities of trust and respect. They want people of integrity. They want managers who actually care about their people. They unknowingly practice our life strategy. They create positive feelings within their cultures.

Studies reveal many highly successful companies naturally align their corporate purpose with our life purpose. They also create a culture that aligns with our life strategy. These attitudes of caring and compassion coupled with behavior patterns creating positive feelings shift these cultures towards states of entrainment, where they increase their odds of finding success.

Personal Leadership:

We all must walk our own path. When others follow, we assume the role of a leader of others. When others do not follow, we remain the leader of our own life. Everyone inherits the role of being his or her own personal leader. Only a few carry the additional role of being a leader of others.

What constitutes a successful personal leader? It closely resembles what defines a person as a leader of others. To be a leader of others you must be walking in a direction in which others also wish to walk. To be a successful personal leader of your own life you must simply be walking in a direction in which you want to walk. Ask the following two questions:

- Am I walking in a direction in which I want to walk?
- Can this direction lead to success?

Just as with leaders of others, successful personal leaders are walking in a direction that aligns itself with their purpose. Their walk reflects their passion, what they care about, what gives meaning to their lives. Their walk also aligns itself with their skills; it must if they are also to walk the path of success. More importantly, successful personal leadership reflects and aligns itself with our life purpose and life strategy.

Innumerable ways exist to align with our life purpose to learn about and practice love. The purposes of those companies listed earlier are only a few examples. Red Skelton, Robin Hood, and the male nurse who works at the hospice where I volunteer are only the beginning of the many ways our professional and personal life can align itself with our life purpose.

Manufacturing, retail and service are the three ways in which people earn a living. Manufacturing builds something for a penny and sells it for a nickel. Retail buys something for a nickel and sells it for a dime. Service provides a service to other people. Sam Walton created an empire in retail; all based on the purpose to "give ordinary folk the chance to buy the same things as rich people."[85] The entire service industry exists solely to help others. Manufacturing creates things to make the world a better place in which to live. Does your purpose align itself with your life purpose? It does if you see and realize how you help others in your daily job and life. Recognize how you help others and you will find that you slowly become proud of what you do.

The heart of personal leadership revolves around its alignment with our life strategy—to create positive feelings in others and ourselves. Our reactions to our environment create our feelings. However, our personal choices usually create our environment.

* * *

Successful personal leadership centers itself on those choices we make that can create either positive feelings or negative feelings. Positive feelings create entrainment that optimizes our odds for success. Negative feelings take us out of our *foresight* brain and place us in our reptilian brain. Our everyday choices have a tremendous amount of control over the positive or negative feelings we have, and this is what personal leadership is about.

We choose what we are going to wear, what we are going to eat, who we are going to see, how we are going to spend our time off. However, our choices go much further. We consistently make choices that determine how we feel. Do you choose to be around people who treat you with respect? Do you choose to apply your free time toward something that makes you feel good about yourself? Do you choose movies and television shows that make you feel good, or make you feel depressed? Do you choose to exercise? Do you choose to give a compliment to your spouse, child, employees or co-workers—or do you only speak when they disappoint you? Do you choose to be a pessimist or an optimist?

Our choices determine whether we go toward events that create positive feelings or whether we go toward events that create negative feelings. For example, I decide to go to a movie. I can choose to go to a movie I know will leave me feeling good or one I know will depress me. That is my choice. I get the opportunity to provide leadership for my life. I have control over whether a simple activity such as going to a movie will create positive feelings or negative feelings. This is personal leadership.

If our life purpose is to learn and practice love, and our life strategy is to create positive feelings, then life leadership is about making choices that adhere to and reflect our purpose and strategy. It is about making choices that lead to creating positive feelings in ourselves and in others.

LIFE PRINCIPLES:

Life Purpose: To learn and practice love

Life Strategy: Create positive feelings in ourselves and others

Life Leadership: Make choices toward positive feelings, not away from them

* * *

Examining the choices that we make on a daily basis reveals we have significant influence on how we feel. Successful personal leadership means making daily choices resulting in positive feelings. Not only do we feel better about ourselves, but we also optimize our chances for success by placing ourselves in a state of entrainment. We have better problem solving skills, better creativity, better intuition, etc. By following our life leadership principle of making choices toward positive feelings, we inherently optimize our odds of being successful in our personal and professional lives. However, successful personal leadership does more.

Emotional intelligence, the ability to become aware of and manage our emotions, builds itself on the foundation of heart intelligence. Not only does heart intelligence serve as the driver to switch our brain and body to either our *foresight* or our *fight or flight* skills based on our choices to create positive or negative feeling, but it also serves as the training ground to make us aware of our feelings sooner in the cycle of emotional responses. It does this through our habit of making choices that will generate positive feelings in our lives. By being aware of what type of feelings our choices create, we actually become more sensitive to our emotions. Practicing life leadership, making choices to create positive feelings, also helps to mature our emotional intelligence.

Life leadership simply means making the choice to walk in a direction toward positive feelings. That's it! Choosing to walk in a direction that creates positive feelings in others and ourselves inherently aligns us with our life purpose and life strategy. Personal leadership is simply about walking in the right direction. It's about choosing to walk toward positive feelings rather than away from them.

Applying the Principle of Leadership

Applying the first principle of purpose to everyday activities means clearly understanding *what* we are doing before we start doing it, while applying the second principle of strategy to everyday activities means clearly understanding *how* we plan to accomplish whatever task we have undertaken or been assigned. Our principles of *purpose* and *strategy* translate into clearly understanding *what* we are doing and *how* we plan to accomplish it.

Our third principle, life leadership, is making the choices that take us in the direction of our life purpose and strategy. It is choosing to walk in a direction to help others and create positive feeling whenever we can. It is choosing to treat others, and ourselves, as we would like to be treated.

* * *

Leadership has an important practical application in our daily personal and business activities. Leadership involves people. It involves the act of someone leading and one or more people following. It is communal. A person makes the decision to go on a diet. This choice is not isolated to the individual. A spouse or friend who keeps urging the dieter to have "just a little ice cream" makes the goal of losing weight harder. Thus, getting the backing and support of the right people becomes critical to the success of almost any activity.

A dieter must ask *who* helps or hinders them accomplish their goal of losing weight, just as a manager must decide *who* makes up the right team for a project.

Without adequate support, business initiatives do not even get a chance to succeed. Hence, whether it is a personal or professional activity undertaken, the logical next step after deciding *what* to do, and *how* to do it, is *who* needs to be involved for the plan to be successful. This is the lesson of leadership, of rallying the people around the vision: determine *who* must be involved and get them involved.

* * *

In everyday life, determining *who* should be involved to help implement the *how* that can accomplish the *what* is the easy part. Getting those people on-board is usually harder. However, the lesson that listening can be more important than talking provides insight on getting the right people involved. In effective communications, when one person truly listens, the sense of empathy that happens increases the odds of a successful resolution being found.

In order to treat people the way you would like to be treated, you must first put yourself in the position of the other person. How else do you truly decide how you would like to be treated? This is empathy: understanding what it feels like to be in someone's shoes. When trying to get someone on-board for an existing plan, chances are high the other person may have needs or desires that you have not considered. Empathy allows us to listen and see needs, scenarios, problems and solutions that our original plan didn't address. Empathy, seeing the other person's perspective, allows a better plan to be created, a win-win scenario that allows the other person to truly embrace a new and improved *plan* that accomplishes the *what.*

In a relationship, personal or business, if one person wins and the other person loses, then that relationship suffers, damaging future interactions. However, practicing empathy—understanding the other person's position and feelings—optimizes the interactions for a win-win solution to emerge. From a purely business perspective, there is no greater business advantage than understanding what your competitor is thinking and feeling.

Knowing what your spouse, your friends and your co-workers are thinking and feeling is the greatest key to creating win-win scenarios and it comes by simply listening and putting oneself in their shoes; it's easy; just make the decision to start doing it.

Having a vision, understanding *who* needs to be involved, truly understanding their needs and views, and then molding the plan or vision so that everyone involved wins, that is true leadership. It's easy for people to support an idea where they win. The key to determining *who* needs to be involved to accomplish the *what* and the *how* consists of finding a common vision or plan for a win-win to occur. It guarantees the people will help, not hinder your actions.

Principle Summary

Successful Living ABCs: Our *attitude* determines the *behavior* that causes the *consequences.*

Attitudes of love, caring, and compassion result in the **Behavior** of treating others the way you want to be treated that causes the **Consequences** that lead to joyful living.

LIFE PRINCIPLES:

Purpose: To learn about and practice love.

Strategy: Create positive feelings in ourselves and others.

Leadership: Make choices toward positive feelings, not away from them.

Worksheet A allows a review of the choices we have previously made by examining our current life situation and choices. Although the worksheet orients itself around four categories (physical, mental, emotional and spiritual), its purpose is to help you review your life and the choices you have made, either consciously or subconsciously. It allows you to determine if those activities and choices lead in a direction toward positive feelings or away from them. Do they support your life purpose and strategy? Feel free to use or ignore the categories listed, but do review and evaluate your current choices and activities to help find out in what direction you have chosen to walk. After completing the worksheets, try this simple exercise for 15 days.

Exercise A: Set aside 20 minutes before you go to bed. Review the choices you made during the day. Grade yourself on whether you made choices that moved you toward positive feelings or toward negative feelings. At the end of 15 days, complete the leadership worksheets again. Do you notice a difference in the direction you are walking?

Principle 3 – Leadership

Worksheet A

Choices: Do the choices you make lead toward positive feelings or away from them? List activities you do in relation to each of the four areas identified. Grade them from 1 to 5, with 1 representing choices you made that created positive feelings and 5 representing choices you made that created negative feelings. Total your score. How do you feel about your score?

Physical: (Do your activities include exercise, getting a massage and eating healthy, or are you a couch potato flipping channels with the TV remote? Etc.)

_____

_____

_____

_____

_____

Mental: (What do you do for your mental health? Do you proactively do things to reduce stress? Do you have hobbies? Do you worry about things you have no control over? Do you slow down at the end of the day before bed or continue working right to the last minute? Etc.)

_____

_____

_____

_____

_____

Emotional: (Are your emotions out of control? Are you a pessimist or an optimist? Do you go to emotional extremes such as rage or depression? Are you mostly happy or sad? Etc.)

_____

_____

_____

_____

_____

Spiritual: (Do you set aside time for inward contemplation? Do you live your beliefs? Are you a hypocrite? Does your faith support you or cause you guilt? Etc.)

_____

_____

_____

_____

_____

Total Score: _____

Section 4 - Management

"Why are we born?" the young boy asked the old man.
"We are born in order to live life," the old man answered.
"Why do we live life?" the young boy asked.
"We live life because we are born," came the reply.

"You have not explained anything but the obvious," thought the young boy.
"Why do you ask questions about the obvious?" thought the old man.

Deep in the heart of a jungle, a team of workers with machetes cut a path through the heavy underbrush. They attack their task, to create a new path to a fresh well of water, with passion. The team consists of Henrik, their leader, Ashka, the manager and six workers. Ashka, a very capable manager, has organized the workers in two groups. A group of three workers cut the underbrush while the other group of three sharpen extra machetes. Setting up a rotation system where cutters rotate with sharpeners to keep fresh bodies cutting with sharp machetes, Ashka's workers are a fine example of organization at its best. After about an hour, Henrik, the leader, decides to climb a tree to measure their progress. Climbing the tallest tree available, Henrik quickly shouts down to Ashka.

"Stop cutting—WRONG direction!

To which Ashka the manager quickly responds, "SHUT UP, can't you see we're making good progress here?"

Leadership is about vision, about walking in the right direction. Management, on the other hand is about execution, about our daily tasks and habits we create to execute our vision. What we do, our tasks and habits, need to reflect our vision. In this section, we explore entrainment guidelines that help establish the right habits to take us toward a successful life. Being a manager is about being a habit helper. Whether it is in managing other people or in managing ourselves, successful management is about helping to create habits that take us toward our vision and reflect our strategy and purpose. This section of Part II reveals our fourth key principle to creating a successful life: management.

Management: A Story

John stood in the doorway of the old farmhouse. A musty smell filled his senses as he walked to open the curtains. The bright sunshine revealed a deserted landscape of old furniture, wood floors, and numerous family trinkets. John grew up in this old house. His parents, now deceased, spent their entire married life here, and it was here in this old house that John's parents had taught him about life.

John had spent most of his adult life not remembering the simple lessons his mother and father had shown him almost every day of their lives. John had a happy childhood. His parents loved each other. His mother loved the small things in life; that's how all the memorabilia got collected. She would tell John and the other children how she got each piece, the location and year of a photograph, and what wonderful or funny event had taken place. Each photo had its own story. John's mother was a natural storyteller. John remembered how he would sit and listen as she told story after story. John's dad would play catch and shoot hoops with John. Both parents worked hard, but mostly they were simple, decent people.

John had done very well for himself, a lovely home and family, yet there was one thing John could not seem to put his finger on. Oh, he tried. Everything he touched turned to gold. The big house, the fancy car, the wife and children, and all the other toys men love so much were supposed to be the key to John's happiness. Yet John somehow never could find the happiness he had known and saw inside the old house in which he now stood.

For that reason, John had come back. He thought that maybe this old house would provide a clue to what he was seeking. After taking a quick look around, he sat down on the old family couch. He remembered his mom telling him and the other children her stories. She said words made the world go around. "Say it enough," she would say, "and it'll come true." As John sat on the old couch, he began to relive his own life. He told people he was going to college to be somebody. He did, graduating near the top of his class. He told people he would be successful and he was. He told people he would marry and have wonderful children and again he had. As John relived his life, he realized his mother was right. "Say it, and it'll come true." In her simple way, his mom understood how this world actually worked. John used words and thoughts all his life to create his world, to obtain that which he sought, yet the happiness he saw in his mom and dad had somehow managed to elude him.

John got off the old couch and began to walk around the living room. He looked at one trinket after another. He went into the kitchen where he remembered the family dinners. He went into the bedrooms and the one bathroom. He even opened the closets hoping to find a clue. He looked through shoeboxes of paper clippings and other frozen moments in time that his mother had saved. None provided the key to his search for the secret to happiness. Disillusioned, John left the old house. The screen-door banged shut behind him as he walked across the porch.

Walking to the car, he became aware of another banging. Looking around, he saw the barn door slamming against the barn frame. *Always something to do on a farm*, John thought as he began the walk to the barn. As he grabbed the barn door, he saw his father's tractor inside the barn. Somehow, John found himself sitting on top of the old tractor where he remembered plowing fields and cutting hay. John had not thought about his father in the old house. Now thoughts of his father flooded his mind.

John's father, unlike his mother, was a man of few words. He was a man of action. He did what needed to be done. Somehow, he seemed to know how to make things work out. After working all day, he would sit on the old porch in his rocker and play his harmonica.

"Enjoy life, son," he told John one day when John was a teenager.

"And how do you do that dad? You're always working on this stupid farm," John shot back at him.

The rocking stopped. John's dad looked him straight in the eye and said. "You'll always have work or some hardship, Johnny. That's what life is about. It's how you respond to that work and hardship. That's what will determine whether you will be able to enjoy life. Won't do any good to get angry at life," he said. "Johnny, you get out of life what you put into it. The good Lord done told us that. You get treated the way you treat others. Remember that and everything else takes care of itself."

Of course, John hadn't remembered. Nevertheless, his dad was right, and John knew it. There would always be something that had to be done, and some hardship standing in front of him. Maybe it was time to start living life like his father had.

John shut up the old barn. He decided it was time to sell the old place and let some young couple who wanted a life of farming have a go at it. John did a lot of thinking on his trip back home. He decided he understood what his mom and dad had tried to teach him. His mother taught him his words and thoughts created the form of the world he lived in. His dad had tried to show him that his choices in the present determined the content of that form.

John did not know how to feel. Life would be even more of a challenge if these were the secrets. He had always made his choices based on making sure his future was secure. Could he change his life so he could treat others like his father and mother had taught him, regardless of how he thought it might affect his future? He realized he had not always chosen love, and sure enough, his future didn't always contain love. Choose love in the present and while you may not know the form of the future, you will know its content—it will contain that which you have just chosen.

Learning the Rules

In all phases of our lives, we learn rules. As children, our parents provide rules that if disobeyed we pay the consequences. In school, we obey the rules or pay the consequences. In society, we obey the rules or pay the consequences of losing our freedoms—we go to jail or lose our drivers license. In sports, we obey the rules or pay the consequences of a penalty.

Knowing the rules makes playing the game easier. Our game, the game of living a successful life, also has rules. The consequences are the results of those rules. Life, however, does not come with an instruction book. We get guidance from those around us, but they too are playing the game without having a set of rules. Each of us discovers bits and pieces. We apply what works and discard what does not work. For me, it was listening to the dying tell me what was important that made me try the same type of experiment as did John Gray, author of the best-selling book *Men are From Mars, Women are from Venus.* I took a new attitude and a new behavior pattern into work and it changed my life. One thing after another began to fall into place. One book after another crossed my path until I understood the scientific reasons why it worked. This section examines the scientific discoveries that show us the real rules of our game. We examine:

- the discoveries by our quantum physicists revealing a new set of rules,

- the rules they discovered and

- how they translate to the everyday rules we need to understand in order to live a successful life.

The rules we live by are not as black and white as we may think. In a court of law, the intent of the person breaking the rules often determines the severity of the consequences. After identifying the responsible party, the person's intents and motives are established. Self-defense is very different from pre-meditated murder, and the consequences are different. The fact that someone's life was taken is not debatable, but the intent of the guilty party often determines the severity of the punishment. Judicial systems worldwide balance the outward facts against one's inward intent.

For our rules of success, we face a similar balancing act. Outward abundance and inward happiness—two complementary aspects in the basic definition of success—are two sides of the same success coin. We must understand both to understand success. The outward concepts of facts and abundance, along with the inward concepts of intent and happiness, form the two sides of our success coin: form and content. There is outward form and inward content, and there are rules that govern each. Thus, we conclude our understanding of our rules by:

- examining form versus content,

- the rules governing form and

- the rules governing content.

Science Provides the Foundation

In 1905 Albert Einstein, at the age of 26, made a remarkable discovery, turning the scientific world upside down. Later, in 1921, he received the Noble Prize for his discovery. It was not his theory of relativity that won him the Noble Prize; surprisingly, it was his understanding of the quantum nature of light.[86]

Einstein showed that light was actually composed of small particles called photons. He showed that when light hit a metal plate, it behaved like billiard balls hitting each other—like particles.[87] His discovery in itself would not seem significant enough to put the world of physics into a spin. However, Einstein's insight into the nature of light, combined with the discovery of Thomas Young some one hundred and two years earlier, was significant. By firing light through slits, Young demonstrated that light behaved like waves, not particles.[88] The upsetting factor about Einstein's discovery was he did not prove Young wrong! Light appears both wave-like and particle-like in nature; yet, this is contradictory.

•

Particle

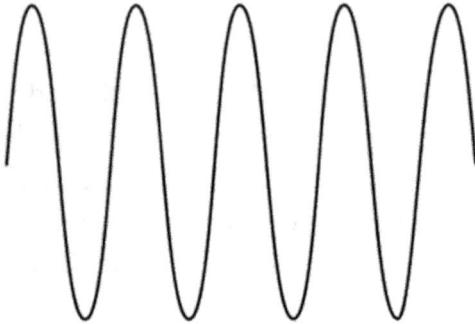

Wave

Niels Bohr would later develop the concept of *complementarity* to explain the dual nature of light—being both particle-like and wave-like at the same time. While waves and particles are exclusive to each other, they do form a complementary relationship, as both are necessary to understand the nature of light.[89] In religion, the nature of the soul versus that of the body would be complementary. They are both quite different and appear to exclude the other, but they are both necessary to understand the nature of a human being.

Gary Zukav, in his overview of the new physics, *The Dancing Wu Li Masters*, describes the significance of these discoveries. Zukav observed that physicists couldn't look at their experiments from purely a black or white perspective anymore. It ended the "Either-Or" view of the world. The concept that light was *either* a particle *or* a wave just didn't work anymore. Light was both and there was no other known explanation.[90]

In 1923, Arthur Compton would push the scientific mystery about duality beyond that of light. Compton used x-rays instead of light to observe *waves bouncing around like particles*.[91] Clinton Davisson and Lester Germer would later fire electrons at a crystal plate and watch in amazement as the *electrons bounced off the crystal like waves*.[92] With particles acting like waves and waves acting like particles, our either-or view of the universe was once again threatened.

Einstein did not help. He proved with his famous $E=mc^2$ (energy = mass times the constant of the speed of light squared) that energy and mass were also just different sides of the same coin. First light, then waves and particles, then energy and mass—our view of the universe as one huge machine made of isolated parts (we being one of the parts) began to melt slowly away in our scientific laboratories.

* * *

Scientists wanted to prove that light was either a particle or a wave. Instead, they had to accept that it was both. They had to acknowledge that light could have contradictory aspects— aspects they labeled as complementary. Our scientific community acknowledged that a relationship existed between waves and particles, just as they had with mass and energy $(E=mc^2)$; not merely a cause and effect relationship, but a relationship in which our ability to group, classify, and neatly put things in their proper place disappeared. The disappearance of the "either/or" way of looking at things means that we have to acknowledge the relationship between those complementary aspects of our world.

Success is like this. Happiness and abundance have a complementary aspect in that happiness represents the content of success while abundance represents the form of success—there is a relationship between the two. Our understanding of each and their relationship to each other forms the basis for our rules. Understanding the rules for success takes into account the complementary relationship that exists between content and form. They are interrelated. Thus, we need to understand their relationship with and how they affect each other, as well as how we affect them, in order to understand what a successful life means.

That content and form are two sides of the same coin is the foundation for our rules. We need to be able to see both sides of the coin and understand the relationship between the two sides. Fortunately, our scientists also had to understand that relationship. They, too, had to discover the rules governing complementary aspects of the same coin.

The Rules for Success

In August of 1939, Albert Einstein sent the President of the United States, Franklin Roosevelt, a letter indicating that uranium could be used to build a powerful new weapon—the atomic bomb. Two months later, Einstein received a polite reply from the President thanking him for his advice, but it was evident that FDR's administration did not believe such a weapon could be built.

One month after Einstein sent his letter to the President, the German Weapons Bureau began work on building an atomic bomb. More than a year passed before the United States took the task of building an atomic bomb seriously. In the meantime, the Germans had more than a year's head start on constructing the most destructive weapon ever imagined. Leading the German effort was the famous Werner Heisenberg, the greatest physicist alive other than Albert Einstein.

Other letters were sent by Einstein, these also politely ignored, while Werner Heisenberg worked dutifully at creating the single weapon that could deliver victory to Hitler's Third Reich—regardless of how Hitler's foot soldiers, tanks, and planes might fare. Hitler's occupation of Czechoslovakia provided Heisenberg with as much uranium as needed to make Einstein's famous equation, $E=mc^2$, work.[93] The Germans' prospect for winning the atomic race was bright.

205

When the Allies of World War II finally defeated Germany, many believe Werner Heisenberg and Hitler were only months away from having a working atomic bomb and rewriting the history of the world as we know it.

* * *

Until I learned of Werner Heisenberg's role in the German effort to construct an atomic bomb, I had known of a different Werner Heisenberg. In his early thirties, Heisenberg began his quest to provide Hitler with massive destructive power. At an earlier age, Heisenberg discovered the "uncertainty principle" in the world of quantum physics. Einstein and Young's discovery of the dualistic nature of light had turned the world of physics upside down. Heisenberg's "uncertainty principle" had been equally earth shattering. Werner Heisenberg, a true leader in the field of physics, was someone whom I admired until I discovered his role in the German effort to dominate the world. Heisenberg, a true follower of Hitler and the Third Reich, transformed from hero to villain before my very eyes.

Or did he? Did Heisenberg really change or did my perspective, my judgment, and my focus towards Heisenberg change? At first, I saw his contribution to the world of physics and admired him. Later, I saw his contribution to the Third Reich and detested him. Most of us have at one time or another known people whom we admired or hated, and over time, came to reverse our position. In many cases, the person did not change and we did not change; however, our perspective and our focus changed. We chose, for some reason, to focus on certain aspects of the person while ignoring other aspects. Even though I know of Heisenberg's discovery of the "uncertainty principle," I still have a hard time seeing him as anything other than the scientific leader of Hitler's attempt to dominate the world. Now I find it difficult to see him also as a great physicist whose contributions continue to open our minds to the true nature of the universe.

My focus determines how I categorize Werner Heisenberg and his contributions to the world. Focusing on his scientific contributions, I see a great leader of new thought and insight. Focusing on his actions as a Nazi, I see the supporter of discrimination and racism. My problem is that I find it hard to see him both ways. I tend to focus either one way or another—I tend to focus on one aspect, but not both.

Oddly enough, the world of quantum physics tells us that it is our focus—our choices as human beings—that determines the manifestation of the physical world. Werner Heisenberg's own "uncertainty principle" proves that we can know either the position of an electron or its momentum (velocity), but not both at any given instant. The more precisely we focus on the position of a particle, the more uncertain its momentum becomes. Conversely, the more precisely we focus on its momentum, the more uncertain its position becomes. As we focus on one aspect, at the quantum level, the other aspect becomes more blurred. However, it is not just that the other aspect becomes more blurred. At the subatomic level, when we observe the position of an electron, we actually change its momentum. When we observe its momentum, we actually change its position. At the quantum level, the act of observation changes the outcome of the experiment—the idea of a neutral independent observer disappears.[94]

* * *

The previous section of this book on leadership illustrates that our choices have a significant impact on our lives. Our focus and choices create the world in which we live. When we focus on art, we become artists, art dealers, or gallery owners. When we focus on automobiles, we become car dealers, race drivers, or auto mechanics.

Just as light has complementary aspects of being both a particle and a wave, the world we live in consists of the complementary aspects of form and content. The "uncertainty principle" suggests we must choose where we want to focus our attention—on form or on content. If we focus on form, then the content becomes uncertain. If we focus on content, then the form becomes uncertain. The law of uncertainty holds true at the quantum level and, from my experiences, it holds true at the macro level of our daily lives. The rules we need to be aware of are:

- Our world consists of form and content.

- If we focus on form, then the content becomes uncertain.

- If we focus on content, then the form becomes uncertain.

Form Versus Content

Happiness and great wealth are examples of content and form in many peoples' definition of success. Great financial wealth, power, or fame represents the outward form, while happiness, joy, or loving and being loved represents the inward content. Yet many of the rich and famous drift into sleep with tears on their faces, excess alcohol in their systems, or hugging a pillow instead of a companion.

We mistakenly believe we find happiness in the form of things. When we get this or that, then we will be happy. Things, in whatever form they take, simply do not make people happy. Becoming rich and powerful does not mean we will be happy—nor does it mean we will be unhappy.

When we focus on becoming rich and powerful, the rules simply say the content becomes uncertain. We do not know whether we will be happy or unhappy because our focus is not on becoming happy. Conversely, when we focus on becoming happy, the rules say form becomes uncertain. We do not know whether we will be rich or poor because our focus is not on becoming rich. However, most people's goal is to experience both happiness and abundance. Fortunately, there is a strategy—not a guarantee—that places us in the optimal position to achieve both.

* * *

We know that lottery winners are no happier six months after they win the lottery than before they won. The American dream of a big house, two or three-car garage (full of course), 2.5 children, a big screen TV and membership in the Country Club will not make us happy—studies show they don't. Happiness is a different side of the success coin. Why do unhappy people who become rich, powerful, or famous remain unhappy, while people who find happiness have a much better chance to find abundance, not only in the physical world, but also in the emotional world?

The answer is simple: when people choose content over form, when people choose to focus on being happy, they tend to create positive emotions that increase their likelihood of also finding abundance. In the first chapter, John Gray's story of deciding to go from seeing eight clients a day down to seven, and treating his wife as his eighth client, not only resulted in a better relationship with his wife and greater happiness, but it also resulted in greater success in his business. He let go of the form (he actually believed his business would suffer) and focused on the content.

When we treat others the way we wish to be treated, we create positive feelings. When we make choices to be happy, we create positive feelings. Positive feelings create heart / brain entrainment. Heart / brain entrainment creates a greater ability to solve problems, find solutions, intuitively know what needs to be done, and create an overall environment for synchronicity to happen. In order to position ourselves to create the *form* we seek, we must first and foremost remain focused on the *content* because it creates the optimal situation in which to excel.

In order to position ourselves to create the form we seek, we must first and foremost remain focused on the content because it creates the optimal situation in which to excel.

This does not guarantee we will create the form we seek. It merely places the odds in our favor. We know our objective, we can create a plan to get there, and by making sure we focus on the content of our actions, we can put ourselves in the best position to execute against that plan.

Focusing on Form

In business, employee motivation is critical to creating highly productive organizations. I once sat on a company committee concerned about employee motivation. The committee members began to devise recognition and reward programs to ensure that each engineer felt important and valued. The committee believed that achieving long-term self-sustaining motivation came from stroking employee egos. Ego, however, represents the form side of the success coin. What represents the content side?

Engineers are only one sector of our society reputed to possess large egos. Managers believe they must stroke those egos to keep the engineering machine running smoothly. Build the ego and build a happy engineer, destroy the ego and destroy the engineer. The problem is that the ego, like a house of cards, can collapse from a single stone thrown at it because the ego-worth individual focuses on form—that outward aspect or image we present to the rest of the world for approval.

A focus on the ego is an expensive undertaking. Managers spend a great deal of time maintaining the egos of ego-worth individuals. Labeled as high-maintenance employees, these individuals also consume a great deal of time building and stroking their own egos, valuable time not spent on being productive. When focused on the ego, considerable effort goes towards maintaining and building that ego.

For these ego-focused individuals, stroking the ego and self-fulfillment are more important than teamwork. Winning and being right are more important than moving forward. Talking is more important than listening. Ego-worth individuals resent it when other less capable people are successful. *The world isn't fair; they should have gotten the award.* The result—they get more angry, more frustrated and more depressed until they quit to go somewhere else where their talents are more appreciated. However, there is a cheaper, faster and better way. Focus on the content of the individual rather than the form.

While *ego-worth* focuses on the form of how individuals obtain their worthiness, *self-worth* focuses on the content of the individuals. What happens when individuals have good self-images of who they are, rather than how they appear to others? These individuals are confident in themselves and do not waste time seeking the approval of everyone around them. They feel good about themselves and tend to create positive emotions within themselves and in others. They do not require huge amounts of care and feeding by management because they are already secure in who they are.

Ego Worth:

- Form focused

- What others think is most important

- Will sacrifice their own values to maintain image / ego

- Dependent on the outside world for their worth

Self Worth:

- Content focused

- Likes who they are

- Likes their values

- Independent and has control over their own worth

* * *

Do you like who you are? Do you like your values? Do you like how you treat others? Do you feel good about yourself regardless of what others may think? These are characteristics of people focused on content rather than form, and these are the people who make an organization successful. Placing yourself or an organization in the best position to be successful means focusing on who you are, not on how others perceive you.

The company committee concerned about employee motivation mentioned at the beginning of this section wanted to implement practices that made employees feel good by stroking their egos, by focusing on the outward form of the individual. A much better plan to increase employee motivation would be to focus on cultivating self-worth rather than ego-worth.

Reward people when they make others successful. Reward teamwork and collaboration. Reward people when they treat others how they would like to be treated. Care about what happens to each other. Preach what is important and practice it. This is how to create self-worth in yourself and in your employees. Stroking the ego of employees is a labor-intensive undertaking.

Focusing on Content

Focusing on form usually brings mixed content. Our state of happiness usually does not change when we obtain riches. Our lives may become easier, but we usually do not grow any happier. However, focusing on content usually brings positive form. This is why our behavior pattern of treating others the way we would like to be treated is critical. Our behavior pattern helps us maintain focus on content. It does not mean we ignore form; it means that in any decision we make, we place content above form. We take the path that tilts the odds of success in our favor.

Looking closely at how life tends to behave, we can create a corollary to the law of uncertainty as follows:

> While our actions and thoughts (i.e., our expressed vision) create the form of our world, our choice of compassion or greed creates the content of our world.

What we see in our mind, we tend to manifest. We talk about it. We do things to make it happen. We chase it down until we hold it in our hands. These are our actions and our thoughts and they become real; they become the form of our future. When we talk about a new car, a new set of golf clubs, or a new dress, in most cases we find a way to make that thing happen. Success declared and a moment of exhilaration experienced and then we are back where we started—

looking for something else to obtain that might bring longer lasting happiness.

Happiness, on the other hand, is not something we purchase, conquer, or obtain. It is something we choose. Each day we all face opportunities to treat others the way we would like to be treated, regardless of whether we judge them to be worthy of that treatment. It is our choice in that moment that determines how we feel about ourselves. It is our choice in that moment that determines who we come to believe we are. It is our choice in that moment that places within us either positive emotions or negative emotions. It is our choice in that moment that determines whether we place ourselves in the situation where the odds for success, for the creation of abundance in our lives, are in our favor. While we may not know what the form of the future will contain, we will know its content—it will contain what we just chose. What we choose determines who we become, not only in the future, but also in the very moment we choose it.

* * *

A simple, single moment in time, called the present, defines who we are. While the present is the consequences of our past behavior and choices, it is also where we determine our future. In our management ABCs, *attitude* determines *behavior* that determines *consequences*. Our attitude *represents content*, behavior *the expression of that content*, and consequences *the form within which we must make our choices that determine our future.*

* * *

Central within Eastern philosophy is the concept of karma. In the West, we understand this concept as cause and effect. Science teaches that something happens which *causes* something else, an *effect*, to occur. In psychology, we use the terms *stimulus* and *response*. In business, sports, and everyday life, we talk of *actions* and *reactions*—something happens that causes an effect, a stimulus evokes a response, or an action causes a reaction.

Events are connected. Sometimes the connection is obvious: driving an automobile too fast around a curve results in the automobile spinning out of control. An overcritical boss can lead to job frustration. Helping a friend in need will lead to feelings of well-being. Separating causes and their associated effects by significant time or distance often results in the cause and effect relationship being lost. When this happens, the West calls it bad luck (or good luck depending on the circumstances). In the East, the relationship remains and is called karma.

When viewed in isolation, labeling cause and effect relationships can be straightforward. Driving too fast results in an accident, the overcritical boss frustrates the employees, the friend feels good because of helping someone. Yet something causes the driver of the car to speed, something causes the boss to be overcritical, and something causes the friend to be helpful.

The driver is speeding because he had a huge argument with his girlfriend. The boss is overcritical because the company is putting undue pressure on her to deliver within unreasonable timelines. The friend helps because someone helped him and he wants to return the favor to the first person who needs help. The cause of our isolated event is actually the result of some previous event, as the result of our isolated event will be the cause of some future effect. The accident causes the driver to take life more seriously, the frustrated employees seek new jobs, the assisted friend decides to also pay it forward to the next person he encounters who needs help.

When seen in isolation, one event is the cause and the resulting event is the effect. When viewed within a larger context, however, each event is both a cause and an effect. The argument causes the accident (the result), yet the accident (the cause) results in the driver taking life more seriously. Niels Bohr's concept of complementarity explains the dual nature of light as being both particle-like and wave-like at the same time. It marked the end of the "Either-Or" way of looking at the world for our quantum physicists. Similarly, the events in our lives are not either a cause or an effect, but both.

We cannot change the past, but in any single event, we will make the choices that determine our future. If *attitudes of love, caring, and compassion* result in the *behavior of treating others the way you want to be treated* that causes the *consequences* that lead to successful living, then it is in the *consequences* of our lives that we find the opportunity to make the choices to change our future. When given that opportunity to choose, do we focus on content, which tends to generate entrainment, or do we focus on form, which often tends to disappoint and create negative feelings?

Attitudes of love, caring and compassion result in the **Behavior** of treating others the way you want to be treated that causes the **Consequences** where we make the choices that determine our future.

* * *

According to the law of uncertainty, choosing content creates uncertainty around form. Uncertainty is unsettling, yet allowing more flexibility in our control over form actually increases our odds for success within the realm of form. Consider the following problem:

Draw three straight lines through all four dots without lifting your pen.

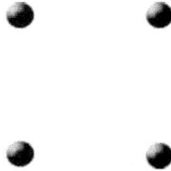

One can quickly solve this problem; consider the following three solutions:

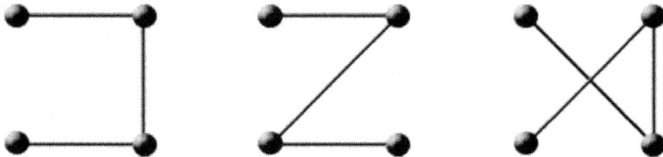

Adding one simple constraint, that your pen must end where it began, causes us to work much harder to solve the problem (answer provided at the end of this section). By placing more constraints on a problem, a smaller number of solutions results.

By not placing constraints on the form of our future, we actually allow an increased number of possibilities for form. Defining abundance as a new house, two cars and membership in the country club restricts our choices of what abundance can be. Why place these restrictions on abundance? The more constraints we put on what abundance must look like, the more difficult it is to achieve. Abundance might be a new house and membership in the country club, or it might be living by the ocean and sailing every weekend. Abundance can come in many shapes and sizes.

New books and techniques teach visualization in order to manifest reality—visualize your new house and being at the country club in order to manifest a new house and membership at the country club. Take note that the key during visualization is to try to feel and experience living in your new home and being at the country club. The activator in these techniques is your *feelings*, not your *thoughts*. Thoughts contain only a fraction of the power of feelings. Classify thoughts as form and feeling as content. It is content—your feelings—that brings manifestation. According to the teaching in these books and techniques, it is the feeling of being successful, the feeling of having wealth, and the feeling of experiencing a wonderful home that manifests those things. The feeling of having wealth is different from the thought of having a specific amount of money. The feeling of having money opens up the possibility of many different amounts of money, or stocks or jewelry. Content does not limit. Form does.

Solution to previous problem:

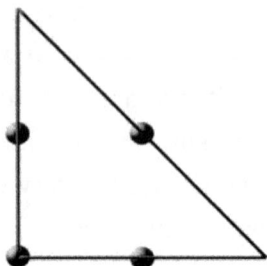

Principle 4: Management

Learning to focus on content above form requires modifying our habits. Creating healthy habits constitutes managing our lives toward the direction in which we are walking. *Leadership* determines where we go. *Management* then becomes responsible for its execution. Management must place one foot in front of the other. The more effectively management can execute, the quicker the objectives are met. Successful management involves creating habits in alignment with our purpose, strategy and the direction established by leadership. Hence, good management is about being a habit helper to ourselves and to others.

Managers and leaders of corporations actually spend very little of their time performing their roles. Both spend the majority of their time fighting fires, the result of a reactive rather than a proactive approach to doing business. Great leaders focus on purpose, strategy, and making sure the entire organization understands and executes the strategy—not fighting fires. Great managers focus on creating the right processes, behavior patterns and habits that adhere to and align with the organization's purpose and strategy. Great managers don't fight fires. Rather, they build organizations that have the right habits so the organization runs itself. They enable workers to make decisions. They create processes enabling the organization to focus on what's important; great managers are habit helpers. They create healthy habits that become an inherent part of the organization and its behavior.

To live a successful life we must be a habit helper for our own life. Life management should align itself with our life purpose, life strategy and life leadership. If our life purpose is to learn and practice love, our life strategy to create positive feelings, and our life leadership to make choices that move us towards positive feelings, then our life management is to create habits that create positive feelings in our lives.

LIFE PRINCIPLES:

Life Purpose: To learn and practice love

Life Strategy: Create positive feelings in ourselves and others

Life Leadership: Make choices toward positive feelings, not away from them

Life Management: Evaluate, modify and create habits that generate positive feelings

* * *

Applying the Principle of Management

At a personal or business level, applying the life principle of purpose means clearly understanding *what* you are doing before you start doing it. The principle of strategy means figuring out *how* you intend to accomplish the task. Leadership means figuring out *who* needs to be involved and getting their support. The principle of management is where you start to *do* the task.

There are two types of activities and behaviors: those that correspond to the strategy—the *how*—and those that do not correspond to the strategy. It is amazing how many organizations and people perform activities that do not correspond to their strategy. They are damaging because they are unproductive and waste valuable time. In some cases they do more than just waste time, they cause negative work.

There are two primary reasons why people or organizations do activities that don't correspond to their strategy. First, they don't have a strategy. Second, the activities are habits—bad habits that need to be broken.

The fast-paced corporate and American lifestyle can create a fire-fighting mentality. As soon as one fire is extinguished, another one needs attention. This hectic approach creates a sense of urgency that overlooks taking a *what, how, who,* and *do* approach. One consequence after another prevents trying to determine and modify the behavior or attitude causing all the fires. In this scenario, taking action and movement makes people feel better. Somebody is doing something about the situation so people feel better, even if it's the wrong thing being done. With no time to think things through, the *what, how,* and *who* doesn't get defined. People are doing things, but they don't correspond to the strategy because there is no strategy. The situation is akin to a system with lots of knobs and switches; turn one and see what happens and keep turning knobs until the right one is found.

The second reason why people do activities that don't correspond to strategy is because many of the activities are habits. Habits are the deep-seated and repeated behaviors of a person or organization. In business, they may be business processes or human processes; in either case, they are the existing behaviors of the people. We do things a certain way, so changing that pattern takes effort.

Back in the early 1960s, a small child asked her mother why she cut off both ends of the beef roast before cooking. Her mother replied that her mother had taught her to cook that way, so that is how she did it. The little girl waited until Grandma came over one day, and then asked the Grandmother why they cut off both ends of the beef roast. The grandmother replied that in her day, the wood burning ovens were too small, so they cut off the ends so the beef roast would fit in the oven. They kept the ends and cooked them the next day. Of course, with the newer modern ovens, there was no need to cut the ends off. The mother had never bothered to question why, it was just a habit.

* * *

Applying the lesson of management means overseeing the activities, behaviors and habits that are being done with the objective to do only those that correspond to the *how* and eliminate those that do NOT correspond to the *how*.

Only do activities that map to your strategy.

We can create, modify or eliminate behaviors and habits, but it requires effort. Doing something 21 days in a row engrains the behavior into your subconscious; you no longer need to think about it at a conscious level. Have you ever started a new job and suddenly found yourself driving to your old work place instead of to your new place of employment? This is why habits and behavior patterns are difficult to form or break—they are deep-seated. It takes a concerted effort to re-wire the brain; fortunately, the next principle reveals the secret to successfully building new behaviors and habits.

Principle Summary

Successful Living ABCs: Our *attitude* determines the *behavior* that causes the *consequences*.

> *Attitudes* of love, caring, and compassion result in the **Behavior** of treating others the way you want to be treated that causes the **Consequences** where choices that determine our future are made.

LIFE PRINCIPLES:

Purpose: To learn about and practice love.

Strategy: Create positive feelings in ourselves and others.

Leadership: Make choices towards positive feelings, not away from them.

Management: Evaluate, modify and create habits that generate positive feelings.

The following worksheets evaluate current habits in order to decide which habits to break and which habits to start.

Worksheet A creates a list of events that evoke positive feelings in yourself when you relive them. Use this list as a quick reference to use whenever you want to shift brain energy from your fight-or-flight brain to your foresight brain.

Worksheet B creates a list of habits you currently have that create positive feelings in yourself.

Worksheet C creates a list of habits you currently do that create negative feelings. These are habits to break.

Worksheet D creates a list of habits you would like to start that would create positive feelings.

Principle 4 – Management

Worksheet A

Positive Feeling Memories: List 10 memories that evoke positive feelings when you recall, focus on or relive them. Note: They do not all need to be in the past—they can be events to which you look forward.

_____

_____

_____

_____

_____

_____

_____

_____

_____

_____

_____

_____

_____

_____

_____

_____

_____

_____

_____

Principle 4 – Management

Worksheet B

Current Habits That Create Positive Feelings In Your Life or Career: *List current habits that create positive feelings:*

_____

_____

_____

_____

_____

_____

_____

_____

_____

_____

_____

_____

_____

_____

_____

_____

_____

_____

Principle 4 – Management

Worksheet C

Current Habits That Create Negative Feelings In Your Life or Career: *List current habits that create negative feelings:*

_____

_____

_____

_____

_____

_____

_____

_____

_____

_____

_____

_____

_____

_____

_____

_____

_____

_____

_____

_____

_____

Principle 4 – Management

Worksheet D

Habits That Would Create Positive Feelings In Your Life or Career: List habits you would like to develop that would create positive feelings:

_____

_____

_____

_____

_____

_____

_____

_____

_____

_____

_____

_____

_____

_____

_____

_____

_____

_____

_____

_____

PART 3: WHY IT WORKS

Section 5 - Culture

"Look deep into nature, and then you will understand everything better."

Albert Einstein

Part 1 of this book showed us how entrainment works and why it plays such a vital role in creating a successful life. Part 2 provided useful guidelines to maximize using entrainment to create more success easily. Part 3 shows why entrainment works and helps us to define more clearly what it means to have a successful life.

The first section of Part 3, Why It Works, reveals our fifth and final key principle to creating a successful life: culture.

Culture: A Story

Martha knocked, but no one came to the door. *Oh Dad, where are you. I need your help,* she thought. She knocked again, repeatedly ringing the doorbell, something she had never done before, but no one answered. Martha turned and while walking back to her car thought, *if Mom were alive, she'd be here to answer.* Not seeing Dad, especially when she wanted—no, needed—someone to tell her everything would be OK was just one more setback to an already frustrating week.

"Martha," her dad shouted just as she was opening her car door.

Martha, looking up, breathed a sigh of relief as her father rounded the corner of the house. If not for high heels and a three-piece business suit with a long tight skirt that prevented anything but short strides, Martha would have run to see her father. Instead, she walked as quickly as she could until her father gave her a big hug.

"Shouldn't you be at work?" her dad said once she finally released him. "Is something wrong?"

"No, yes… no," she began. "Yes, I should be at work and no, nothing's wrong. Well, not life threatening."

"But something is wrong?" he said.

"Oh, Dad, it's just been one of those weeks, ah, months at work, and I just need to talk. That's all," she said while thinking, *if you don't help me I'm going to lose my new job as President of S-Core, which means my career is dead!*

"I was just working in the garden out back. Come on in. I'll get you some iced tea and we can talk."

After settling down on the back porch of a two-story 1960s house that Martha's dad and mom had renovated into a modern showcase, Martha slowly began telling her dad that work was a mess. She was hired only four months ago to save S-Core, a once up-and-coming company whose innovative product line had become stale. The founder, who was the CEO and Chairman of the Board, hired Martha to breathe new life into the company, giving Martha her first shot at running a company.

"Dad, if I don't figure out how to turn this company around, my career will be dead. No one will hire me again."

"I'm willing to listen," her dad replied, "but I don't know anything about business, honey. I was a college professor of psychology. Not exactly someone schooled in the hard knocks of business."

"Dad, I think I know the problem, I just don't know how to fix it. Nothing in school or business has ever taught me how to fix this type of problem."

"So what's the problem?" her father asked.

"It's complicated. Well, maybe not complicated, but definitely not the usual issues."

"How so?" her father asked.

"Dad, before, my job was mostly to increase productivity. You know, optimize things. You might trim this department, increase staff in another, kill this product line, you know, the typical optimizing where you are spending or saving money. Then, there's also optimizing the people and departments once you figure out staffing or budgets. That's not too hard as there are lots of business process improvement techniques. I use Six Sigma for manufacturing and business process, CMMI for software …"

"Hold on, kid," her father interrupted. "I don't know all these buzz words and acronyms you're starting to spit out."

"Oh, sorry," Martha replied. "It doesn't matter. What matters is that there are sound process improvement techniques to figure out how to save a penny here and there when it comes to figuring out the best process to use to get something done. If I can figure out how to do something in four steps instead of six steps and maintain or improve quality, I can save a lot of money."

"So what's the problem? Honey, you've done this before; don't you feel you can do it here at S-Core?"

"Dad, here's the catch. S-Core's money issues and business processes are not the problem. The business processes are not that bad. Sure, I can get the experts to improve them to save some more money, but that won't save the company; that's a common mistake managers make. If you just make the company efficient, then it should work out. It doesn't. Recent research shows that of 58 large Fortune 500 companies that implemented Six Sigma programs—Six Sigma, that's a popular business process improvement technique—

that a full 91% have failed to keep up with the S&P 500 in the stock market."[95]

"Can I get a list of those companies, sweetheart? I want to make sure my money's not invested with them," her father joked.

"Dad, it just goes to show that improving business processes can save you some money, but it's not what makes you money. S-Core's problem is that it is not making enough money. Shaving some dollars here and there in order to make the numbers work will not save this company. Remember, you told me that in the 1950s schoolchildren were taught to get under their desks in case of a nuclear attack. Trying to make the numbers work for S-Core is similar. It's not going to save the company; the problems are way bigger."

"So what is the real problem?" her dad asked.

"There's no creativity, no innovation, no new products. The R&D efforts just keep tweaking and improving their old products. The market is passing them by."

"So you need to get the company to be more innovative, more creative?"

"Right," Martha said. "But I don't know how to do that. School and business haven't taught me to do that. They've taught me how to balance budgets, improve process, and provide leadership, but they haven't taught me how to make someone more creative."

"Have you tried?" her father asked.

"Yes, but I'm failing, big time!" she said.

241

"Go on," her father said.

"Today I fired one of the main managers," Martha said. "He was yelling and cursing at one of his employees in front of a large group of people. I felt so sorry for the employee. I looked into it. The employee hadn't done anything major. She could have done it better, but she didn't deserve the treatment she received from the manager. But it's not just this manager. The entire company is fear based. Managers routinely intimidate and bully the employees. It's not hard to figure out why there's no innovation and creativity: everyone's too scared of getting yelled at, bullied, or even fired, so they play it safe. I guess I didn't help by firing the manager today, but I had warned him several times that I wouldn't tolerate that type of behavior.

"It's worse," Martha continued. "The CEO found out and called me into his office; really gave it to me hard. Bottom line, I'm on a very short leash to get this company turned around or I'm on the unemployment line."

"Doesn't HR have all kinds of training programs to help with this type of problem? You know, team building, motivational techniques?" her dad asked.

"Dad, you know as well as I do, those programs rarely make any lasting changes in people. Sure, they are full of wonderful information, but somehow, three months later it's just the way it was before the training ever happened.

"I even got together with the process improvement experts, even called in consultants, but when they asked what I wanted to improve and I said 'creativity', they just shook their heads. Creativity isn't a business process."

"Ah, I think I see why you're here," her father said. "You have a fear-based organization. That fear is killing creativity and innovation. The fear comes from the behaviors of your managers; you need to change the human behaviors. You might say the human processes are what you need to address."

"Right," Martha replied. "I realized that. I also realized that business and process improvement experts don't know much about modifying human behaviors—business processes, yes, but not human processes."

"But I do," her father replied.

"Yes, I figure a psychology professor should know something about modifying human behavior."

"What do you want to know?"

"Let me first tell you what I've done and maybe you can tell me what I'm missing," Martha said.

"Ok, it sounds like you already have started on this. Tell me what you've done," her dad replied.

"I decided to start with my own team of managers," Martha began. Martha went on to tell her father she believed that creating a positive work environment might be a good starting place to figure out how to change human processes. If she could do that, she might be able to figure out how to attack generating more creativity and more innovation. Martha had discovered that most Americans receive negative feedback, but little or no positive feedback. A full 65% of American workers actually receive no positive feedback at all within a work year[96]. Hence, she simply asked her management team to take the opportunity to give out positive feed-back to employees whenever the situation arose.

"After a week," Martha began, "I asked the team how they were doing with our experiment. Dad, do you know what their reply was? They said 'With what?' They didn't even re-member we were going to focus on giving out positive strokes. We talked about it and everyone agreed that we needed to do it. We all believed it could help.

"The next week I again asked how everyone did and guess what? I got the same 'with what' reply. Two weeks and none of us really changed our behavior, even though we all wanted to.

"I don't get it Dad; it shouldn't be that hard to start a new behavior pattern. Especially when everyone believes it will help the organization."

"Don't be too hard on yourself, honey," her father said. "It's actually very hard. How many people are successful at their New Year's resolutions? Very few, and it's because of the same reason you've run into. Come look at my garden."

"Dad, I don't want to see your garden now. I want an an-swer."

"The answer is in the garden. Now come on."

They walked back to her father's garden in the corner of the lot.

"You know," the father began, "it's organic. I don't use any pesticides to kill the weeds. I could spray and it would save me a lot of work, but then it wouldn't be organic."

244

"It looks very nice," Martha said.

"Yes, but it takes a lot of work to keep the weeds out. If I let the weeds get in, they compete for the water and minerals and it could ruin my little garden. But I don't. You know what it requires. I have to come out here almost every day and inspect the garden to see if there are any weeds. I have to constantly watch my garden to ensure I catch the weeds before they can do damage."

"I don't understand, Dad. So you have to watch out for weeds in order to keep your garden in good shape."

"I wouldn't if I used pesticides. Just spray occasionally and no weeds and not a lot of effort on my part either. Your organization is similar to my garden, except it's not organic. It's using pesticides when it comes to changing human behavior patterns. Just asking people to behave a certain way isn't likely to cause a change. Think about it for a minute, sweetheart."

Martha paused but didn't seem to make a connection. Then a smile suddenly began to appear. "Watching. That's it, isn't it? You have to inspect your garden every day to make sure it's the way you want it to be. Because you don't use pesticides, if you miss a few days of watching, the weeds are back. Breaking or creating new behavior patterns are the same way. They need someone or something to help watch over them until the behavior is firmly established."

"That's right," her dad began. "To create a new behavior pattern, you have to reward or reinforce the desired pattern so it can become engrained into your subconscious. You currently have no reward or reinforcement mechanism in place to

GABRIEL LAWSON

help your managers engrain the new behavior. Actually, you do. It's just that the rewards and reinforcements that are in place are currently rewarding and reinforcing the fear and bullying that is already the established pattern."

The next day Martha went to work with a new excitement. She met with her team. They all agreed they needed help in remembering to hand out positive comments. They decided to have Martha's assistant come by at the end of each day to collect how many positive strokes they gave out each day. They formed two-person teams and Martha gave out rewards each week for the two-person team that gave out the most positive comments. Knowing that someone would actually check at the end of the day provided the gentle reminder the team needed to start a new behavior pattern. It started slowly, but the constant *watching* was just the helping hand the managers needed to establish the behavior pattern in their subconscious. After a while, it became natural; it became a habit. The team of eight managers gave out over 8000 positive strokes to their team in the next six months.

More importantly, Martha and her team realized that it was the existing human behaviors—the human processes—that created the fear-based environment preventing creativity and innovation. They examined the existing behaviors, identified the desired behaviors, and created reward structures and the support mechanisms—the watching—that allowed the organization to rid itself of bad behaviors, replacing them with new behaviors that encouraged and supported innovation and creativity. It wasn't long until several new product lines were introduced, catapulting the company back into the

246

news. Martha didn't lose her job; instead, she received a rather sizable bonus for her work.

Choosing Our World

Our main strategy for creating a successful life is straightforward: choose to create and maintain heart / brain entrainment. Encouraging heart / brain entrainment creates the optimal state for success and abundance to occur.

Our success ABCs show us that the first step is creating and living with an attitude of caring and compassion. A behavior pattern of treating others as we would like to be treated reflects and reinforces the proper attitude while creating habits that naturally bring entrainment into our lives. Finally, it is in the present moment that our choices between content and form determine our future. Our ABCs are a structured formula that leads to a more joyful and successful life. Sometimes it takes an act of faith to apply that formula.

In my case, it took repeated messages from the dying and others to convince me to embrace it. Even then, I felt my decision would be the downfall of my climbing the corporate ladder. Others have discovered this formula in one form or another and for many it took a life-changing event to make them change their attitudes, behaviors, and choices. Sometimes simply knowing the formula is not enough for people to embrace it. To help embrace the formula, it sometimes helps if we understand *why* the formula works, not just *how* it works.

Negative emotions cause our heart and brain to get out-of-sync. Our key to success, entrainment of our heart and brain, disappears when we allow fear, greed, anger, etc., to root and grow within our being. Positive emotions such as love, caring, and compassion place us in a state of heart / brain entrainment that increases our creativity and problem-solving abilities, our intuitive abilities, and our tendency to be in the right place at the right time. What is more elusive is why heart / brain entrainment works. We know it works—studies prove it works. We know how to make it work, but why does it work?

* * *

The discovery that our world is not an "either/or" world forced our quantum physicists to change their thinking. Previously, they were able to neatly classify each element of our world and put it in its place, neatly tucked away on the appropriate shelf in this laboratory called life. Discovering that light is both a particle and a wave, not simply one or the other but both, forced our quantum physicists to change their understanding of what equality means. To understand why entrainment works, we also must change our view and understanding of how the universe works.

A particle is the same as a wave—both are the representation of light. Light is not the only place where a new understanding of equality appears. Einstein's $E=mc^2$ shows that energy and mass lie on the opposite sides of the equal sign. Energy and mass are not two separate things. They are different representations of the same thing, two sides of the same coin.

Our ABCs also show us a fuller, more comprehensive meaning for some of the things we have classified and neatly placed on a shelf in our life laboratories. Intelligence is much more than IQ. It also includes emotional and heart intelligence. Feelings influence much more than our emotional state. They are the keystones for creating or destroying entrainment. Form does not sit on one shelf and content on another. The uncertainty principle indicates that they are intertwined.

To understand why entrainment works, we must expand our view to see our world not as an "either/or" world, but where sometimes apparent contradictory aspects exist together as different faces of the same entity. We examine the complementary aspects of separateness and wholeness to see that the individual and society are two sides of the same coin called life.

We already know the concept of separateness: we exist in a perpetual state of viewing our world as a collection of individual pieces. On the other hand, what do we know about wholeness? What have our scientists discovered about the other side of the coin? To see how these aspects relate to our success, we examine:

- how history has shaped our view of separateness and wholeness,

- what the prophets have taught in regards to these concepts and

- what our scientists have discovered that shows ours is not an "either/or" world, but a world of both separateness and wholeness.

We will see that our team is much larger than we think, and that there is a smarter way to accomplish our goals. We will gain a deeper understanding of what it means to do less and accomplish more.

Heart / brain entrainment works, and if we can understand why it works, we can let our bird out of its cage. We can overcome our biggest obstacle: finding the courage to adapt our thinking to the truths our scientists and other new pioneers are uncovering.

What History Tells Us

From the dawn of man up to the middle 1600s, a period of approximately three million years, which I will call the *ancient mystic* period, men mostly lived as hunters and gatherers, existing much on the same level as the animal kingdom. Life was a continuous search for food and shelter. Fire, and in particular the invention of agriculture some ten thousand years ago, would eventually separate man from beast. Instead of a day-to-day search for food, man could store food for a rainy day—and the keepers of the food became the rulers. Kingdoms grew and eventually spread over most of the earth allowing humankind to defeat the animal species in the battle for dominion of the earth.

The *ancient mystic* period enjoyed a limited oneness with the earth and the heavens. Each tribe, culture, and civilization considered itself a part of a greater whole. They did not understand the whole, thus the name *mystic*, but they did behave accordingly. Gods ruled the world and man obeyed the gods. Not pleasing these gods resulted in punishment; above all, the notion that something greater than man was "out there" permeated man's thoughts and actions.

Everything under the heavens was alive. The earth and the universe were living, breathing entities. Merlin, the wizard from King Arthur legend, referred to the earth as the dragon.

The dragon, if commanded by the gods, could open itself up and swallow whole villages. It could spit fire and create new islands. It could sweep in and blow away homes. It could land and shake the world with its weight. The dragon was alive and man lived along side it as ruler of the animals. Above all, the notion that man, the earth, and the gods were all part of one organic creation ruled this period of humanity.

The human race understood its separateness from the universe, but the understanding was from a perspective that humankind was a part of a greater whole, a living breathing intelligent whole that man was subservient to but also of which he was a part.

* * *

More free time came as agriculture spread, time for man to think and resolve the mysteries of the universe. Science slowly began to take root and spread. In the 1500s, Copernicus put forth his theory that the earth revolved around the sun. Humanity could and would not accept this, as is true with most new ideas, but it marked the beginning of the second great period in our history—the *scientific* period. If the earth was not the center of the universe, then man was not a part of some great creation. Instead, as Newton would later emphasize, man was an isolated part of a large lifeless machine. The universe became mechanical; no more dragons breathing fire, only man and the elements—alone, isolated, insignificant, left to fight the elements with his wits and whatever weapons he could create.

Knowledge became king. With knowledge, humankind could understand how the universe worked and then put it to work. We no longer spoke of an organic universe, of the concept that man and the universe were connected, or that we worked in parallel with that universe. We spoke less of God and more of uncovering the truth about our universe. Humankind sat silent while our scientists conducted experiments in their white coats and sterile laboratories, silently observing and witnessing with objectivity the outcomes of their investigations. For 400 years, we have watched and silently waited for science to reveal the mysteries of the universe to us. In the meantime, we have gone about making our lives more comfortable. We have invented machines to do work and entertainment to fill our senses.

Somewhere along the way, our understanding that we are part of a greater whole disappeared. The pendulum of understanding both wholeness and separateness swung all the way to the side of separateness. Our scientists took wholeness, removed its life, removed its soul, and left us with a mechanical universe of one gigantic clock ticking away without concern or care about the inhabitants of that universe.

It is easy to understand separateness, but the understanding of wholeness can be easily lost. We live and breathe separateness, but wholeness is harder to see, hear, and touch. The teachers of wholeness have disappeared over the last 400 years, so we have no one to tell us about the mysterious dragon our ancestors understood. Instead, we have our scientists trying to finalize their great experiment. For the last 400 years, we have waited patiently and silently for our scientists to put the final additions on the mysteries of this great machine, but those final changes are beginning to un-ravel the great machine.

What Our Prophets Say

Treat others as you would like to be treated. This is the essence of the wisdom of Christ, Gautama Buddha, Lao Tsu, Mohammad, Gandhi, and other great prophets in our history. We know this simple behavior pattern creates entrainment that enhances our ability for success. Our prophets taught a basic behavior pattern that, when practiced, brings success. Millenniums later, our medical and social scientists discovered the concept of entrainment and verified the common sense teaching of the prophets. The prophets knew the simple life secrets our scientists are only beginning to understand. Are there other secrets too in the prophets' teachings?

In their teachings, we find a second major theme. In Christianity, we find the simple teaching "for whatsoever a man soweth, that shall he also reap" (Galatians 6:7). In other religions, we find the concept of karma: we reap what we have previously sown. This concept is much more basic than the concepts of salvation or enlightenment. This concept explains at a very basic level why it is important how we treat each other. According to the prophets and religion, how we treat each other is how we will be treated. If we wrong our brother, we will be wronged. If we love our brother, we will be loved. If we help our brother, we will be helped. Thus, if we want success, then we should help others be successful. If we want abundance, then we should help others with their abundance. If we want happiness, then we should help place a smile on our brother's face.

In the eastern concept of yin and yang, yang is seen as more masculine, taking more action, or being hotter, while yin is seen as being more feminine, being more at rest, or being cooler. Each thing is classified as either yin or yang depending on its relationship to another object. For example, man is yang when compared to earth, but yin when compared to Heaven.[97]

The Chinese symbol illustrating the yin/yang concept depicts a flowing togetherness not found in our Western mechanical view of dualism. Part of each exists in the other—as represented by the small dot of white found in the black region, and the small dot of black found in the white region:

Yin and yang are different sides of the whole. Both are required to understand the Universe, as is the wave/particle aspects of light in the understanding of light. We cannot be *either* yin *or* yang; we are *both*. Hence, our focus needs to include the whole, not just the concept of separateness. At the quantum level, Bohr's concept of complementarity parallels this Eastern concept. Both force us to pull away from the concept of things being separate and more towards the acceptance of things being parts of an integrated whole.

Nevertheless, our western view tends to focus on the individual aspects of the whole rather than on the whole. We see hot and cold, not temperature; we see black and white, not color; we see soft and hard, not texture; we see man and woman, not humankind; we see heads and tails, not coins. To see reality and how it works, we need to see the world of temperature, color, texture, humankind, and coins—not the individual elements of those things.

* * *

The reason we reap what we sow, according to the yin/yang concept, is that we are not individual gears, wheels, and pieces in a giant unconscious clock, as our Newtonian view of the world has taught us. We are, according to the yin/yang concept, all part of one harmonious whole. Light is not *either* a particle *or* a wave, it is *both*. We think we are separate entities that at best have a cause and effect relationship with other entities, but our prophets are telling us that we are much more. We are a part of an integrated whole and that explains why we reap what we sow. If we pinch our left hand then we feel that pinch. Our left hand is not a separate piece, detached from our self. It is a part of our being, just as we are a part of a larger whole. Our prophets teach that we reap what we sow because we are nothing more than a left hand of something larger than we are. We are not separate from it. We are a part of it.

Behind the teaching of our prophets lies a concept of wholeness, not separateness. Could our prophets again be right? Could their simple concept of yin and yang show that while there is an appearance of things being separate, things are actually pieces of one integrated whole, just as our left hand is a part of the integrated whole we call our body?

History shows us that our scientists nailed the lid on the coffin of wholeness, firmly solidifying our perspective that we are merely cogs in a giant lifeless clock known as the universe. However, our quantum scientists, the rebels of the scientific world, are removing the nails in the lid covering our understanding of wholeness.

What Our Scientists Tell Us

Heart / brain entrainment enhances our problem solving abilities by providing more clarity and insight, but it does this in a non-scientific way. It enhances not only our clarity, but also our intuition and synchronicity, areas relatively foreign to science. Scientists are now addressing these issues, not because they want to, but because their investigations are leading them down a path that simply will not allow their dismissal.

In the world of quantum physics, scientists, in order to explain what they are observing, are asking a very unscientific question: "How does the universe know?" Albert Einstein started it and many have followed by concluding the universe is intelligent and we are a part of that intelligence, not a separate cog in a great unconscious machine. Einstein and his cohorts are bringing us full circle to what our ancients taught us, but this time it is science, not mysticism, carrying the torch.

At the turn of the 20th century when our quantum physicists began to make the final additions to the great machine, Albert Einstein added one too many final changes. He turned the scientific world upside down with his discovery of the particle aspect of light. With Thomas Young's earlier discovery that light was a wave—which Einstein's particle discovery did not disprove—the foundation for light's dualist nature crushed our "either-or" way of looking at the world. This contradicted the basic assumptions of the *scientific* period.

Einstein and Young's separate discoveries about light started a wave of investigations that would eventually shake the very foundation of the scientific world. Thomas Young passed sunlight through two vertical slits to show interference, a characteristic of waves. Scientists would later shoot a single photon through one of two slits and record evidence we are still struggling to accept. A single photon can only go through one slit, yet it behaved as a wave if the second slit (which it did not go through) was open and behaved as a particle if the second slit (which it did not go through) was closed. Scientists had to ask the question, "How did it *know* whether the second slit was open or closed?"

The *scientific* period, led by Copernicus and Newton, painted a picture of man as an independent part of the universe. We were small independent wheels within a great machine and each part was either a gear or a spring or a some other identified unique part. The dilemma of the duality of the nature of light—combined with Arthur Compton, Clinton Davisson, and Lester Germer's proof that this complementary concept encompassed many aspects of our world, not just light— awakened within the scientific world a new mystery. No longer was their job to keep breaking down the elements until they revealed the smallest building blocks of the great machine. Scientists now had a real mystery on their hands. How does the universe know whether the second slit is open or closed, especially when the photon doesn't go through that second slit? The second slit should be independent of the experiment. As scientists began to attack this mystery, they also attacked our role within the universe as previously defined during the *scientific* period.

* * *

Batting second in our lineup of scientists swinging at the foundation of our Newtonian view of the universe was Werner Heisenberg, the German physicist who delivered a crushing blow with his discovery of the "uncertainty principle". Heisenberg showed that the neutral observer in the white coat behind the glass barrier changed the outcome of the experiment simply by the act of observation. When we measure the position of an electron, we modify its momentum. When we measure its momentum, we modify its position. The problem is that the change is not due to the intrusion of our measuring devices. It is in the nature of the universe that our act of observing causes the modification. The importance of Heisenberg's discovery was that we no longer could stand by in a white coat observing scientific experiments. We became a vital part of the experiment itself. We couldn't watch without influencing the outcome.

In the world of physics, the concept of the Universe as one big machine—and we and everything else simply cogs, wheels, or gears within that machine, each performing a single job—began to disappear. Our physicists gradually began to discard the idea that we could be independent observers of our world; rather, we were a vital part of a wholeness that did not allow for independent cogs and wheels. The either-or view of the world began to give way to a concept of wholeness and completeness.

The finishing touches the scientists were supposed to provide had undermined the whole foundation built by Copernicus, Newton, and other scientists of the *scientific* period. The new scientists were unconsciously taking sides with the mystics and our prophets. The either-or concept was giving way to the complementary aspects of yin and yang and separateness was giving way to wholeness.

* * *

The third batter in our lineup of scientists swinging at the foundation of our Newtonian view of the universe came from the field of psychology. Sigmund Freud matured the concepts of the conscious and the subconscious. He would later join forces with a young psychologist by the name of Carl Jung, considered by many to be the greatest psychologist of the 20th century. Jung, however, became disillusioned with Freud and dissolved the partnership to work on his own. Carl Jung's work would lead him to define and mature the concept of the *collective unconscious*.

According to Jung, the *collective unconscious* is something greater than our combined individual conscious and subconscious. Freud saw the subconscious as being composed of individual experiences that had been forgotten by the conscious. Jung's *collective unconscious* did not come from our individual experiences, but from something greater than the individual. Jung saw a wholeness in the collective unconscious.

A *collective unconscious* does not fit our world-view of a human being as a separate entity, existing apart from the rest of the universe. Somehow, the *collective unconscious* indicates man is not isolated; there is a type of consciousness greater than that of the individual. While Einstein and his cohorts were beginning to paint a picture of wholeness and wondering about the intelligence of the universe, Jung painted a picture of an intelligent universe via a collective unconscious.

* * *

Einstein would again step to the plate and deliver a hit against the Newtonian view. He, Boris Podolsky, and Nathan Rosen proposed a thought-experiment.

Electrons have the appearance of spin—either up or down, or right or left. A twin pair of electrons will have opposite spins. If one spins up, the other will spin down. If you change the spin of one, then the other will automatically change its direction to maintain an opposite spin. Now here is the trick. If you separate them, say by the space of an entire galaxy (this is why it was a thought experiment), if one changes spin, the other will also immediately change its spin. The Einstein-Podolsky-Rosen experiment left the scientific community wondering how one electron could be aware of the spin of the other electron over such a long distance. Science says it is not possible to transfer information that fast.

To communicate information requires a carrier, a signal, and nothing can travel significantly faster than the speed of light. So how can information get across the galaxy at speeds faster than light, at the speed of thought?

It was only a thought-experiment and it pushes us toward answers we might not be prepared to accept. Nevertheless, experiments using polarization by John Clauser and Stuart

Freedman along with experiments by Alain Aspect proved Einstein's thought experiment. All of this led to its mathematical proof known as Bell's theorem. Gary Zukav called Bell's theorem a Trojan horse as it requires what appears as telepathic communications and forces physicists to investigate phenomena in which they do not believe.[98]

Our scientists hint that we are not isolated pieces within the universe. We actually change the outcome of an experiment simply by observing it. The universe is not a set of independent pieces. A wholeness exists that is intelligent and passes information around at the speed of thought. Science indicates Carl Jung's *collective unconscious* has a basis within the physical science of quantum mechanics.

Random Coincidences and Small Miracles

In the *ancient mystic* period, permeating man's thoughts and actions was the notion that something greater than man was "out there." Thanks to the discoveries of emotional intelligence and heart intelligence, we see that we are more than a rational mind. Thanks to the discoveries by our quantum physicists, we see that we are more than an individual. Heart / brain entrainment integrates our rational brain, our emotions, and our feelings to aid us in accessing the collective unconscious—the vast information system our scientists now recognize as an intelligent universe.

Our scientists offer the theory that something greater than man is "out there" and man is part of that greater something. Man and the universe are an integrated part of the same intelligent thing—man's thoughts, actions, and decisions are responsible for the way things are. Because we are a part of an integrated intelligence, we are not isolated from it. We are a smaller part of an organic system of information passing. Section 2 presented two studies reflecting this expanded concept of wholeness. The first involved twenty-four cities that experienced a reduction in crime when as little as one percent of the city's population participated in meditation. The second demonstrated that women who were trying to become pregnant, when prayed for by strangers, were twice as likely to conceive as the group of women who received no prayers.

There exists a wholeness and connectivity in our world that exceeds our understanding, but which our scientists are now beginning to see, not only within our social and physical sciences, but also in our biological sciences. DNA studies reveal that DNA strands constrict and expand respectively when exposed to situations that create negative or positive feelings. Additional studies prove that DNA taken from a subject and transported hundreds of miles away still constricted and expanded when the subject was exposed to situations that created negative and positive feelings.[99]

We are a part of a larger organic system with an advanced information passing system—we are part of the *collective unconscious* of an intelligent universe. We are on a very large team and our challenge is to let that team do work for us. We need to use the universe and its information to accomplish work for us. We do this when we acknowledge more than the rational mind as key to our success. By expanding our thinking beyond seeing success as us against the world, we see the world as working with us to bring success. This opens the way to "do less and accomplish more."

On the other side of the coin, we benefit when we help and enable others. Reaping what we sow means that when we enable others, we are enabling ourselves. If we want success, then help others be successful.

* * *

Why do the prophets teach us to treat others the way we want to be treated? Why do they teach us that we reap what we sow? Knowing our scientists are beginning to see our universe as the mystics of old saw it—as an integrated intelligent whole—we understand why we reap what we sow. We reap what we sow because our left hand is not separate from our body. We are not separate from the larger body our scientists are now beginning to call the intelligent universe. If we are a part of it, what we do unto it we also do unto ourselves.

In Section 1, I wrote about Dannion Brinkley, a man whom I had never met. His near-death story helped give me the courage to try an experiment at work that would help lead to my understanding of success. The very weekend after I wrote those pages, my wife and I accidentally met Dannion Brinkley in my hometown in Colorado—Dannion lives in South Carolina. I was finally able to thank him for how his life had affected mine although our worlds are thousands of miles apart. Is it random coincidence that I would meet this man the very week after I wrote about him—or was it the integrated intelligence of the collective unconscious at work? When we begin to understand, acknowledge, and believe in an intelligent universe, we begin to notice and experience our expanded team in our daily life. Small miracles and acts of random coincidence happen more often. Ours is an intelligent universe and we are a part of that collected wholeness. In the national best-selling book series, *Small Miracles,* there is story after story about events too great to ignore.

A man, out of the blue, decides to depart from his traditional walk home and take a different route. He comes upon a man attacking a woman. Somehow, he finds to courage to attack and fight off the assailant. The woman, now crouched behind a tree, turns out to be his daughter. [100]

A sad, lonely, and angry old man lost his entire family in a Nazi concentration camp. He shows a stranger, his chauffeur for the day, the tattoo bearing his identification number. He explains his father, mother, himself, and his brother got increasing consecutive numbers when they entered the concentration camp before the Nazis killed the rest of his family. Surprised, the stranger informs the old man that it is a coincidence that the number on the old man's arm is only one digit different from his last four digits of his own social security number—the number that would correspond to the old man's younger brother's number. He explains that he recently met another man with a number tattooed on his arm—the exact same number as the last digits of his social security number. The older man miraculously reunited with a brother he believed to be dead because another man had met someone whose tattoo coincidently happened to be the same as the last digits of his social security number. [101]

A church blows up at 9:10 a.m. on Sunday morning, apparently killing all twenty members of the church choir—except for the first time in twelve years of choir practice, all twenty choir members showed up late, missing the explosion that would have killed them. [102]

Principle 5: Culture

Our physical, biological, and social sciences are all finding evidence of an intelligent universe. They are proving that we are not isolated and alone in our struggles. Our previous four principles of purpose, strategy, leadership and management focused inward at our own values, desires and choices. Our fifth and final principle looks outward at how the outside world either helps or hinders our ability to have a successful life.

Our final principle recognizes we are a part of something greater than ourselves. Recognizing that life is not an either / or situation, but that separateness and wholeness are both sides of the same coin, our final principle for creating a successful life looks beyond our individual self. It looks outward at those around us. It looks at the culture and the community in which we choose to live, and how they either support or hinder our objectives.

Our outside world, our culture or community in which we choose to live, plays a vital role in our quest for a successful life. We are not alone. Our friends, co-workers and family contribute to the management of our lives.

Our *life leadership* principle asks that we make a conscious choice to walk toward positive feelings. We make that choice because we know that our life strategy comes from creating positive feelings that place us in a state of entrainment, which optimizes our skills, creativity, and intuition, thereby increasing our odds of success in whatever we are undertaking on a personal or professional level.

While our *life management* principle evaluates and challenges us to create habits that help create positive feelings, our *life culture* principle asks us to focus outward to examine, evaluate, and change, if needed, the community in which we live in order to create a support environment that helps, not hinders, our quest for a successful life.

Friends, family, and co-workers contribute to our feelings. Our choices in friends should be ones that support our quest. Are they positive people? Do they support us? Do they contribute to our walk toward positive feelings or do they continually complain and point out all the negatives in every situation? What about co-workers and family; do they support our quest or are they a hindrance in creating positive feelings? If not, we do have choices. Choosing to find new friends, change jobs, or get a divorce, are extreme, but they are viable choices. I moved from a large city where drive-by shootings were becoming commonplace to a smaller city with family values because I wanted a better place in which to raise my newborn daughter. Sometimes our best choice is to get rid of the old and replace it with something new, but there are other choices.

Employers sometimes fire people. Rarely is it because they do not have the skills to do the job. Usually, detrimental behavior or the inability to work with others is the reason why most employers get rid of an employee. For example, the desire for job security often causes employees not to share information with others, or a person's unwillingness to compromise on ideas or approaches suggested by other team members creates environments unsuitable for acceptable productivity. Most states require that before releasing these people, the company implement a corrective action plan to help modify the behavior causing the problem. Behavioral modification, according to B.F. Skinner's behaviorism theories, happens by providing rewards for the desired behaviors. They can be either positive rewards or negative rewards. Losing your job is an example of a negative reward.

Our friends, family and co-workers are all candidates for behavioral modification techniques. Suppose a friend continually gossips, talks badly about others, or is always creating a drama around the most minor of events. Providing support is a vital part of being a friend; however, excesses in certain behavior patterns are not good for our friends or us. We could choose to find a new friend or we could find a way to reward new behavior or set boundaries.

Suppose we decide to stop the habit of gossiping about others. Our friend is not helping as his or her behavior only fuels the fire. One option is to tell our friend of our decision to stop gossiping; that we are more than willing to talk about lots of things, but not about other people in a negative way. When it happens, acknowledge what is going on to each other. This way, both parties become coaches or helpers for the other party. Create a game to see who first notices when gossip starts. Another option is to change the topic of conversation whenever it shifts towards gossip. Over time, the other person will subconsciously realize that you are not a good person with whom to gossip. Another option is to excuse oneself and leave. Our most drastic option is to find a new friend; however, finding a new friend may be the option we need to follow if all else fails. This is a difficult option.

Whether it is our personal community or a corporate culture, we, as managers of our own life or as managers of others, cannot ignore our responsibility to evaluate, and, if necessary, try to change the culture and community in which we choose to live and work.

Our life *purpose* is to learn and practice love. Our life *strategy* is to create positive feelings. Our life *leadership* asks us to make choices that move us toward positive feelings. Our life *management* principle requires us to fashion habits that create positive feelings in our lives. Our final life principle, *culture*, requires us to choose and create a supportive and positive environment in which to live.

LIFE PRINCIPLES:

Purpose: To learn about and practice love.

Strategy: Create positive feelings in ourselves and others.

Leadership: Make choices towards positive feelings, not away from them.

Management: Evaluate, modify and create habits that generate positive feelings.

Life Culture: Create a supportive and enriching culture

David H. Maister's criteria for high-achieving corporate cultures indicate that successful corporate cultures are in alignment with our life strategy to create positive feelings. Whether it is our personal life or our professional life, the culture with which we surround ourselves greatly influences our lives. We can choose in which parts of our current culture we will participate and in which parts we will not. We can choose to reward or not reward certain behavior patterns in our friends, co-workers, bosses, employees and family members. Skinner's behaviorism theories prove that we can and do have the ability to modify the behavior of those around us. If we cannot, we also have the ability to choose to change the landscape of the community. We can find new friends, new jobs, even a new place to live, but we do have the choice and the ability to modify our environment so that it aligns with our principles for a successful life.

Applying the Principle of Culture

The practical application of the life principle of culture comes from realizing that we are not separate from the universe. There is an intelligence that is larger than we are; hence, our responsibility as the manager and leader of our lives is to step beyond our own abilities and use the talents and abilities that we are being offered. Our responsibility is to acknowledge and accept help.

Any task we undertake starts with clearly understanding *what* we are doing, *how* we intend to accomplish it, *who* needs to be involved and getting them engaged, and then *do* only those activities and behaviors that correspond to our strategy. *What, How, Who,* and *Do:* a simple strategy that optimizes our chances for success. However, the next step, that of applying the principle of culture, guarantees we have done our best to accomplish our task.

Culture is the behaviors and values of a group of people. Peer influence goes a long way towards molding behaviors and values. Whether or not we are consciously aware, Big Brother, in the form of culture, constantly watches over us, molding our behavior to fit into the accepted patterns. It watches and continually reminds us of the expected behaviors. Culture punishes members that do not behave accordingly and rewards members when they do.

This same watching and modifying of behavior is the key to successful project management: create a plan, *watch*, and when things go astray, correct them. In project management, managers or project assistants are dedicated to *watch* in order to verify the work is being accomplished. In our everyday life, we usually do not have an assistant to verify that the work we are doing is actually accomplishing the plan we have put in place. We must take on that responsibility.

Our behaviors are critical to how successfully we accomplish our tasks. Our behaviors and habits support or hinder our execution. Thus, we need to work to implement behaviors and habits that help, not hinder, our goals. However, the hard part of creating a new habit is not doing the new behavior 21 days in a row; the hard part is *remembering* to do the new behavior. *Watching* is the key to remembering.

Culture says that we are part of a larger team, and that team can and will help us. That team can and will help *watch* our behaviors, but we first need to ask for help. Without help, most New Year's resolutions fail.

Take the example of wanting to stop gossiping about people. It takes someone with a strong will to say that he or she is going to quit a long-standing activity and then successfully do it. The new behavior starts for a few days, but it does not take long before it is forgotten and the old habit is as strong as ever. However, consider the person who asks his or her spouse to ask every night at dinner who he or she gossiped about that day. Having to face a real person with admission of undesirable behavior day-in and day-out creates awareness. This constant reminder gradually causes awareness to shift from dinner to a time nearer to when the actual event happens. Adding a phone call from the spouse at lunch to say hello and ask "how's it going with the gossip thing" allows the person to remember the new behavior. Sticky notes in an organizer for meetings with friends who are fellow gossipers can help. Twelve step programs and accountability groups or partners are also examples of this technique.

Watching is the key to creating new behaviors. *Watching* is the key to verifying whether the activities you are doing are accomplishing your plan. *Watch* what is happening and take corrective action.

Determine *what* you are doing, *how* you intend to do it, and *who* needs to be involved. Then *do* those activities and behaviors that correspond to your strategy, and *watch* the results to take corrective actions. Sounds simple. It is. Just do it.

* * *

Principle Summary

Successful Living ABCs: Our *attitude* determines the *behavior* that causes the *consequences*.

> **Attitudes** *of love, caring and compassion result in the* **Behavior** *of treating others the way you want to be treated that causes the* **Consequences** *where choices that determine our future are made that lead to joyful living.*

LIFE PRINCIPLES:

Purpose: To learn about and practice love.

Strategy: Create positive feelings in ourselves and others.

Leadership: Make choices toward positive feelings, not away from them.

Management: Evaluate, modify and create habits that generate positive feelings.

Culture: Create a supportive and enriching culture.

* * *

The following worksheet provides a mechanism to evaluate our culture and community. Evaluate your professional and personal cultures and determine what changes will help bring them into better alignment with your purpose and strategy.

Principle 5 – Culture

Worksheet A

Positive Culture Evaluation: Evaluate your culture. Is it a culture that assists in creating positive feelings or one that encourages negative feelings? Create an action plan for how you can change those situations that create negative feelings.

_____

_____

_____

_____

_____

Worksheet B is a continuation of worksheets C and D from the previous principle—Management—where you identified both negative habits you wish to get rid of and positive habits you wish to create. In order to successfully create or break a habit, the key is *remembering* to do the new behavior. This involves *watching* your actions to see if you remember to do the new behavior. For each habit you listed in worksheets C and D of the previous section, determine a plan for how you will watch your actions to see if you are remembering to do the new habit each day.

Principle 5 – Culture

Worksheet B

Watching Plan for New Habits: For each new habit you wish to create, determine how you will watch and evaluate your actions during the day to determine your progress. Examples: (A) Review your behaviors for the day with your spouse after work during dinner. (B) Get a buddy that wants to create / break the same habit and create a competition that is reviewed each day. (C) Schedule a time in your day-planner for a 15-minute review.

Habit:

_____

_____

_____

_____

Watching Plan:

_____

_____

_____

_____

Section 6 - Conclusion

A patient man does not wait.
An impatient man always waits.

Having a successful life isn't about money, cars and houses—the traditional items we often associate with success. While successful living may bring these physical items, a successful life goes deeper. From the dying, our ancestors and from new scientific discoveries comes a message showing that real success comes from who we are, not what we own. It comes from the content of our lives, and in a successful life, content always precedes form. Meaning, fulfillment, satisfaction and happiness comprise the criteria we use to make our final judgment of our lives. The entrainment factor shows that creating positive feelings place us in the optimal state to achieve success. We have control over the choices that define who we are, and it is in those choices that we create a successful life.

Conclusion: A Story

The following story is the retelling of a popular folktale attributed to Huai Nan Tzu.

In a time far from the present, an old farmer's horse ran away. The farmer's neighbor, having heard of the event, went to speak with the old man.

"It is a terrible thing that has happened," said the neighbor. "That was your only horse which you depended on to grow your crops and make your livelihood. How will you survive? What will you do? This is surely a stroke of bad luck," the neighbor said to the old man.

To which the old man replied, "Who knows what is good or what is bad?"

The neighbor, taken aback by the old man's response, reiterated to the old man that it was indeed a bad thing. The old man, unshaken by the events or by the neighbor's perspective, simply replied, "Maybe, maybe not."

The neighing of horses awoke the old man the following morning. Arising and looking outside, he saw not only his own horse, but also an entire herd of wild horses that had followed home the horse that the old farmer worked, fed, brushed and loved.

News of the old farmer's good fortune spread quickly through the village and, by early afternoon, the neighbor returned to express his relief and happiness to the old farmer.

"This is surely a grand event. You will be a wealthy man now," the neighbor told the old farmer as they sat on the old farmer's porch admiring the corralled herd of wild horses.

Yet the old farmer seemed unmoved and simply replied, "Who knows what is good and what is bad?"

The neighbor, being a somewhat logical man, insisted this was indeed a good thing and in time, the old man would come to understand and see the error of his attitude and eventually realize this as a true stroke of good luck.

To which the old farmer replied, "Maybe, maybe not."

The next day the farmer's son began to tame the wild horses. He successfully mounted and rode a number of the horses. Shortly after noon, as he mounted a beautiful black stallion, he was thrown from the wild horse. As he hit the ground, a sharp pain in his leg indicated he had broken his leg. That afternoon, the neighbor again visited the old farmer to express his regrets over the son's unfortunate accident.

"I am sad to hear of your son's unfortunate accident," the neighbor said.

"Yes, I am sad my son is in pain," the farmer replied.

Finally, thought the neighbor, the old farmer understands the meaning of good and bad luck. "Yes," the neighbor stated, "It is unfortunate such a thing has happened."

"I said I was sad for my son's pain, not that it was an unfortunate event. I do not know if this is a good thing or a bad thing that has happened to my son," the old farmer said.

"You have gone too far this time. Surely you must see from the pain your son suffers that this is not a good thing," the neighbor replied.

"Maybe, maybe not," was all the farmer would add.

Dejected at both the unfortunate fate of the farmer's son and his inability to make the farmer understand the obvious, the neighbor said his goodbye and went home.

When the neighbor returned home, a messenger for the King greeted him. The King wanted the neighbor to assemble all the able-bodied young men to go fight and defend their country from an invading army from the east. The neighbor knew that many of the young men would not return, as they would fight bravely, but they would be greatly outnumbered. He immediately thought of the farmer's son; having a broken leg, he would not be able to go fight, thereby saving his life. *The old farmer just doesn't realize how lucky he really is,* he thought. In the back of his mind, he could clearly hear the voice of the old farmer saying, "Maybe, maybe not."

Living a Successful Life

Robert, the head of Marketing for a Fortune 500 company, aggressively recruited a younger "hot shot" in a rival company. Robert and his team toasted each other with tinkling glasses full of bubbling champagne the day Robert convinced the "hot shot" to come work for him. On top of the world, with a promising future of success—now that he had landed the last and strongest ingredient for his team—Robert drifted into sleep that night feeling unbeatable; success was finally his. For the next six months, success followed success. Robert, at the zenith of his career, knew the late nights and weekends were worth it. His boss arranged an evening dinner at an exclusive downtown restaurant with Robert and himself. Robert knew he would be receiving a promotion and a substantial pay-raise.

Praise for Robert and his landing of the "hot shot" flowed from the boss's lips as smoothly as the expensive wine slid down Robert's throat. Light-headed, Robert laughed when the boss told him the "hot shot" was so good he could do Robert's job. When the boss's smile turned upside down, Robert's sobering realization that the boss wasn't joking hit Robert like the chilling, blowing rain when stepping outside on a cold Chicago night. From the heights of success to the depths of failure within the span of time it takes to eat a meal, Robert's grand idea to lure the "hot shot" to his team was now his downfall. It was not the success to which he once toasted champagne.

Robert did not believe life could get lower until he walked through the building with a cardboard box packed full of his personal belongings. The people who once hung on his every word watched in silence as the security guard escorted Robert out the doors he had opened for eight years. That day the doors closed behind him for the final time.

Failure or success? Ten years later, Robert recounts with laughter and amusement the story of how his boss wined and dined him only to drop him as Betty Anderson, his high school girlfriend, did the summer before his senior year. As a result of being fired, Robert launched his own company and it became an immediate success. Without that "kick in the pants" as Robert refers to it today, he would never have had the courage to step out on his own. Today, Robert says the best thing that ever happened to him was being wined and dined and booted out the door.

* * *

A number of years back I had to close the doors to one of our small development shops in Atlanta. The company had failed to sell the product this small group produced. The ten employees saw all their hard work and impending layoffs as a failure. Within one month, each employee had found a new job, all with increased pay; one woman had increased her pay from $30,000 to $50,000. Was this failure or was this success?

Our view and definition of success and failure is very much like cause and effect—it is hard to determine what is what until the end comes. It is much like Werner Heisenberg's own "uncertainty principle" in that, as we focus on placing the label of success or failure on a particular event or objective, we do not see the big picture. When we do see the big picture, it becomes difficult to label an event as either a success or a failure. Perhaps it is easy to label it as both when we see the big picture. To label it as one or the other becomes more difficult when we place it in perspective with the other successes and failures, or causes and effects, in this event called life. Perhaps it is only at the end, when we have judged all of our successes and failures, when we have closed all of the doors we are to close, when we are breathing our last breath, that we will really be able to judge success.

* * *

When we look at life, at our successes and failures, we see that success, like most things in life, is a process and our judgments about the events in our lives change as our lives progress. This is life: a series of perceived up and downs, of perceived successes and failures. More than anything, it is our judgments that determine whether we declare something as a success or a failure.

For me, and I assume for many of you, the outside world, the mysterious "they"—the people who make the rules—are the ones I let determine what success looked like. When I was a child, it was my parents; as a teenager and then a college student, it was my peer group; as an adult, it was corporate America. They told me what the form of success should look like. I worked hard to achieve that form and I discovered that I gave up a lot in order to claim success. Only when I let go of somebody else's view of success and began to define my own criteria for success did I finally begin to feel successful—

not appear to the outside world to be successful, but to actually feel successful.

A man walks across a street, trips and falls as he steps on the curb. The outward form of the man's actions is not debatable. However, what was happening on the inside, what the man was feeling or thinking as he walked across the street, is unknown to everyone but the man. In order to declare success, we must feel successful. Whether we appear successful is actually irrelevant. Appearing successful is the outward form. It satisfies the ego; it provides ego-worth. How we feel on the inside reveals the content, the self-worth.

Common to each perceived success or failure in our lives is our ability to choose, in that moment, who we are. We define the content of our lives, not by the outward form it takes, but by the inward content we give it. Those choices do not cost anything. They do not require luck, or being born into wealth, or winning the lottery or working until midnight every night. We make those choices whether we want to or not. We are forced in each moment of each day to define who we are.

It is hard to control the world and how the form of our world comes into being. We hire the "hot shot" as our savior, only to learn that our hiring of her was our downfall. One moment, the form of the world appears to be going our way; the next moment it is not.

* * *

On the other hand, the content of our lives and who we are is entirely under our control. We get to make the choices that determine who we are each and every day. This book has tried to show that by focusing on those choices, we actually create the most optimal environment for success to happen.

A simple strategy of "treating others as yourself" creates positive emotions. Positive emotions, according to the rules, create the optimal environment to solve problems, find solutions, and intuitively know the next step. Negative emotions, according to the rules, do the opposite. By focusing on who we are, on the content, we develop not only the emotional intelligence needed for success, but also the right attitude that determines the behavior that produces the consequences of our lives.

Most people focus on the form rather than the content. The job title, salary and window office become more important than the content. Somewhere, sacrifices are made, and as we sit in the window office, our feet on the corner of our desk, our title on the outside of the door, we begin to wonder if it was worth what we gave up to get here. Little Johnny batted over .300 in Little League. At least that's what Johnny's mother told us. We were too busy working late at night to go to most of his games. Mary looked so grown up, like a princess, when she went to the senior prom in her purple dress and hair pulled up like Audrey Hepburn. At least that is the way she looked in the photo—we were out of town on a business trip the weekend she went.

By focusing on the form, we place constraints around that form and overlook the choices that appear before us that define who we are. When we focus on content, we release the constraints on form. As content becomes more important than form, form becomes free to follow content. Success is then free to come in many different forms—not only the one fixed into our image of what success has to be. Amazingly, we may be surprised how abundantly the form may manifest itself.

* * *

So what does it mean to live a successful life? When success is at the cost of sacrifice, then what we have done is to trade one thing we hold dear to us for another. To climb the corporate ladder at the expense of a marriage is not success. No, it is simply a trade, a bartering of one set of goods for another.

Success is achieved when you experience life's ups and downs, life's perceived individual successes and failures, as a statement of who you are. When you choose to give to someone because that is who you are, not give up something because you want something in return, that is when you create the environment for success. Giving is different from giving up something. Treating someone the way you would like to be treated is different than treating someone a certain way because you want something from him or her. When you do not see what you do as a sacrifice, but as an expression of who you are, then you have reached a successful life. The form that manifests itself does not come with sacrifice. It comes from a freedom only a focus on content can provide. It comes without catches, without sadness and without regret. It comes easily when the choices we make are a reflection of our true self.

* * *

Donald, a chief scientist at a large corporation; Thomas, a president of a corporation; Jonathan, a hat maker; Mary, an artist; Ellen, a factory worker; John, a train conductor; William, a program manager; and Sally, a real estate agent; all passed through my life on their way to closing the final door of their lives. It was when they faced death that they were able to see the final big picture and make a final judgment about the success or failure of their life. We will all get that opportunity.

Dannion Brinkley, the man whose near-death experience gave me the courage to change how I approached my work and my life, has had two additional near-death experiences. In each of Dannion's three near-death experiences, he tells of a 3-D life review that happens when we die. These life reviews are not an argument for life after death; but they are an argument that we will experience a life review at the time of death. What happens or doesn't happen after the life review is not a part of this book.

The life review experience, such as the ones Dannion had, has been documented by thousands upon thousands of other individuals all over the world who have died and been brought back to life. This part of the near-death experience is now universally recognized. For the individuals who experienced it, they have their beliefs as to what it means. To the doctors and scientists who try to explain it, they theorize that it is the final shutdown of the brain. Just as we dream at night and create worlds that seem as real as our waking world, so too can this experience be the creation of the brain.

Regardless of whether this life review is the beginning of an after-life or the final shutdown of the brain, it is something that each of us will experience. It will be our final judgment on the success or failure of our lives. Dannion describes his first life review as not that pleasant. He had mistreated many people and found himself not only experiencing his own feelings but also the feelings of pain and humiliation that he caused the people he mistreated. In his life review, he literally received exactly what he had sown. But it didn't stop there. Dannion found himself experiencing and feeling the pain of the next person in a chain reaction that his actions had started.[103]

He tells of an incident when he was in Vietnam when he was assigned to assassinate a Vietnamese colonel. Dannion tells of squeezing the trigger and then seeing the colonel's head explode. In his life review, he first felt what the colonel felt: confusion and sadness with the realization he was dead and would not see his family again. Then he began to experience the feelings of the chain reaction he had started: the sorrow of the colonel's wife when told of her husband's death and then the sadness of his children. He saw each of the people he had killed as part of his service to his country in the same manner, experiencing the horrible feelings his actions had created.[104]

However, these experiences of reaping what he had sown did not apply only to his actions towards people. He also tells a story of what he experienced when he simply helped make a transfer of weapons to military interests in Central America. In life, he helped transfer guns at a military staging area. In his life review, he continued with the guns, experiencing the results for which the guns were used: children crying when finding out their dead father would not be coming home because of the guns Dannion helped to deliver. According to Dannion, the results of the actions of the first part of his life were horrible.[105]

Fourteen years later, Dannion would suffer a heart attack and experience a near-death experience for a second time. In this life review, he again experienced the first twenty-five years of his life just as he had in his first life review, but the next fourteen years were different.

Dannion's life review was different because his life was different. Dannion's new life consisted of helping others, of volunteering at hospice and at nursing homes. He felt the other person's gratitude when he did such simple tasks as helping people stand or brush their teeth. Even the smallest of actions that helped others brought pride for having made better choices in his life. Living a good life of creating positive feeling in others, according to Dannion, is like watching fireworks at the Fourth of July, only you feel the wonderful emotions and feelings you have created in others.[106] Dannion understands what it is like literally to reap what you sow. It is why, if you ever hear him speak, his mission is to create as many good feelings in others as he possibly can. At your life review, when you get to make a final judgment on the success or failure of your life, you get to experience all the wonderful feelings that you have created in others.

Our life review is not just from our perspective. It is from the other person's perspective. How we treated them is what we feel when we experience our life review. New meaning arises from our behavior pattern of treating others the way we would like to be treated. We actually experience how we treat others, so in essence, how we treat others is exactly how we treat ourselves. For each act of kindness we do for someone, we get to experience the feelings it brings to that person; and for each act of meanness we commit, we also get to experience what that feels like. How we treat others is, in the end, how we treat ourselves.

Does the near-death experience mean there is a life after death? Maybe, maybe not. The universal acknowledgement by such a large number of people who experienced a near-death experience tells us one thing of which we can be certain—we will experience it. It will be our last time to judge success and we are asked to judge it from the perspective not of form, but from the actual choices we made during our entire lives. The last thing we will ever do is to judge, not merely our work, but our entire lives; and it is from the perspective of how we treat others that we get to do it. This may be the last feeling we ever have and then again—maybe, maybe not.

Acknowledgements

I would like to think all the men, women and children at hospice who passed through my life on their way to another world. To them and their families I extend my blessing and gratitude. Without their constant message about the real meaning of life, I would never have changed my life or discovered the powerful mysteries of the heart. For it is in my heart that I find the treasures of my life: to my loving wife, Rebeccea, and my loving children, Bethany, Ashley, Lori, and Danen, I extent my thanks and love.

I also extend a huge thank you to my editors. It is through the guidance and expertise provided by Deb Cartwright, Karen Moe, and Danen Jobe that this book now finds itself in your hands.

Lastly, I extend thanks to you the reader. For it is you who give life and meaning to a set of words.

Reference and Notes

[1] Gray, John. *Men are From Mars, Women are from Venus*. New York: HarperCollins Publishers, Inc. 1992. p. 188.

[2] James, Michael S. *Can't Buy Happiness, Study Finds Money Last Among Psychological Needs; Self Esteem in Top Four*. ABCNews.com, February 11, 2001 http://abcnews.go.com/sections/living/DailyNews/happiness01021 1.html (Retrieved 2010-04-22) From: Kennon M. Sheldon, Andrew J. Elliot, Youngmee Kim, Tim Kasser, *What is Satisfying About Satisfying Events? Testing 10 Candidate Psychological Needs*, Journal of Personality and Social Psychology, Feb 2001, Vol. 80, No. 2, pp. 325 – 339.

[3] Lao Tsu. *Tao Te Ching*. translated by Gia-Fu Feng and Jane English. United States: Vintage Books, 1997. Verse Forty-Two.

[4] Zukav, Gary. *The Dancing Wu Li Masters—An Overview of the New Physics*. New York: Bantam Books, 1980. p.92.

[5] Sun Tzu, Translated by Thomas Cleary. *The Art of War*. Boston: Shambhala Publications, Inc., 1998. p. 1.

[6] Samuel Crowther's interview with Henry Ford, World's Work, 1926, pp 613-616.

[7] Robinson, Evan. *Why Crunch Mode Doesn't Work: 6 Lessons*. http://archives.igda.org/articles/erobinson_crunch.php. 2005. (Retrieved 2010-03-04).

[8] Robinson, Evan. *Why Crunch Mode Doesn't Work: 6 Lessons*. http://archives.igda.org/articles/erobinson_crunch.php. 2005. (Retrieved 2010-03-04).

[9] Lao Tsu. *Tao Te Ching*. translated by Gia-Fu Feng and Jane English. United States: Vintage Books, 1997. Verse Forty-Two.

[10] Spoken statement (c. 1903); published in Harper's Monthly (September 1932)

[11] Kübler-Ross, Elisabeth and Kessler, David, *Life Lessons*. New York: Scribner, 2000. quote p. 11.

[12] The benefits of entrainment are taken from:
Heartmath Research Center, *Science of the Heart*, compiled by Rollin McCraty, Mike Atkinson, and Dana Tomasino, Institute of Heartmath, Publication No. 01-001, Boulder Creek, CA, 2001.
Neurocardiology - Anatomical and Functional Principles, J.Andrew Armour, Publication No. 03-011, Institute of HeartMath, 2003.
The Appreciative Heart - The Psychophysiology of Positive Emotions and Optimal Functioning, Rollin McCraty and Doc Childre, Institute of HeartMath, 2003.
The Energetic Heart - Bioelectromagnetic Interactions Within and Between People, Rollin McCraty, Institute of HeartMath, 2003.

[13] Dava Sobel, David. *Galileo's Daughter*, United States: Walker Publishing Company, Inc.

[14] Capra, Fritjof. *The Tao of Physics*, London: Flamingo, 1992. p. 17.

[15] Braden, Gregg. *The Isaiah Effect*. New York: Harmony Books, 2000. p. 246.

[16] Brinkley, Dannion with Perry, Paul. *Saved by the Light*, New York: Villard Books, 1994. pp. 3-7, 22-23, 50-58.

[17] Brinkley, Dannion with Perry, Paul. *Saved by the Light*, New York: Villard Books, 1994. pp. 20-21.

[18] Kübler-Ross, Elisabeth. *The Wheel of Life*. New York: Scribner, 1997. p.191.

[19] Collins, James C. and Porras, Jerry I. *Built to Last* (paperback). New York: HarperBusiness, 1997. p. 228.

[20] Collins, James C. and Porras, Jerry I. *Built to Last* (paperback). New York: HarperBusiness, 1997. table 11.1, quote p. 225.

[21] Collins, James C. and Porras, Jerry I. *Built to Last* (paperback). New York: HarperBusiness, 1997. table 11.1, quote p. 225.

[22] Collins, James C. and Porras, Jerry I. *Built to Last* (paperback). New York: HarperBusiness, 1997. table 11.1, quote p. 225.

[23] Collins, James C. and Porras, Jerry I. *Built to Last* (paperback). New York: HarperBusiness, 1997. table 11.1, quote p. 225.

[24] Collins, James C. and Porras, Jerry I. *Built to Last* (paperback). New York: HarperBusiness, 1997. p. 227.

[25] Collins, James C. and Porras, Jerry I. *Built to Last* (paperback). New York: HarperBusiness, 1997. p. 224.

[26] David H. Maister, David H. *Practice What you Preach – What Managers Must Do To Create A High Achievement Culture.* New York: The Free Press, 2001. quote p. 162.

[27] Collins, James C. and Porras, Jerry I. *Built to Last* (paperback). New York: HarperBusiness, 1997. table 11.1, quote p. 225.

[28] Childre, Doc and Martin, Howard with Beech, Donna. *The Heartmath Solution.* United States: HarperSanFrancisco a division of HarperCollins Publishers, Inc. 1999. p. 38.

[29] Childre, Doc and Martin, Howard with Beech, Donna. *The Heartmath Solution.* United States: HarperSanFrancisco a division of HarperCollins Publishers, Inc. 1999. p. 6.

[30] Childre, Doc and Martin, Howard with Beech, Donna. *The Heartmath Solution.* United States: HarperSanFrancisco a division of HarperCollins Publishers, Inc. 1999. pp. 242-244.

[31] Childre, Doc and Martin, Howard with Beech, Donna. *The Heartmath Solution.* United States: HarperSanFrancisco a division of HarperCollins Publishers, Inc. 1999. p. 14.

[32] Goleman, Daniel. *Emotional Intelligence.* New York: Bantam Books, 1997. p. 149 references: The study of 250 executives: Michael Maccoby, "The Corporate Climber Has to Find His Heart," *Fortune*, (Dec. 1976).

[33] Goleman, Daniel. *Emotional Intelligence.* New York: Bantam Books, 1997. p. 149 references: The study of 250 executives: Michael Maccoby, "The Corporate Climber Has to Find His Heart," *Fortune*, (Dec. 1976).

[34] Braden, Gregg. *The Isaiah Effect.* New York: Harmony Books, 2000. p. 236 references: "Maharishi Effect: Increased Orderliness, Decreased Urban Crime," *Scientific Research on the Maharishi Transcendental Meditation and TM-Sidhi Programs: A Brief Study of 500 Studies,* Maharishi University of Management Press (Fairfield, Conn.: 1996, 21.)

[35] Natural Health Magazine. *Article: Praying to get pregnant? New science says you may get an answer.* April 2002, p. 25. (Note: Article indicates researchers at Columbia University in New York City performed studies that were published in September 2001 in the *Journal of Reproductive Medicine*).

[36] His Holiness the Dalai Lama and Howard C. Cutler. M.D., *The Art of Happiness.* New York: Riverhead Books, 1998, p. 126.

[37] Childre, Doc and Martin, Howard with Beech, Donna. *The Heartmath Solution.* United States: HarperSanFrancisco a division of HarperCollins Publishers, Inc. 1999. p. 11.

[38] Childre, Doc and Martin, Howard with Beech, Donna. *The Heartmath Solution.* United States: HarperSanFrancisco a division of HarperCollins Publishers, Inc. 1999. p. 12.

[39] Childre, Doc and Martin, Howard with Beech, Donna. *The Heartmath Solution*. United States: HarperSanFrancisco a division of HarperCollins Publishers, Inc. 1999. p. 12.

[40] Goleman, Daniel. *Emotional Intelligence*. New York: Bantam Books, 1997. pp.34-36.

[41] Goleman, Daniel. *Emotional Intelligence*. New York: Bantam Books, 1997. p. 35 provides the following references and notes: George Vaillant, *Adaptation to Life* (Boston: Little, Brown, 1977), The average SAT score of the Harvard group was 584, on a scale where 800 is tops. Dr. Vaillant, told Daniel Goleman about the relatively poor predictive value of test scores for life success in this group of advantaged men.

[42] Goleman, Daniel. *Emotional Intelligence*. New York: Bantam Books, 1997. p. 35 references: J. K. Felsman and G. E. Vaillant, "Resilient Children as Adults: A 40-Year Study," in E. J. Anderson and B.J. Cohler, eds., *The Invulnerable Child* (New York: Guilford Press, 1987).

[43] Goleman, Daniel. *Emotional Intelligence*. New York: Bantam Books, 1997. p. 35.

[44] Goleman, Daniel. *Emotional Intelligence*. New York: Bantam Books, 1997. p. 46

[45] Reagan, Nancy, *The Eternal Optimist*, Time Magazine, June 14, 2004, Vol. 163, No. 24.

[46] 1980 FBI Statistics, *Murder Circumstances/Motives*. http://pegasus.cc.ucf.edu/~surette/tvent.html. 1980. (Retrieved 2010-04-011).

[47] Childre, Doc and Martin, Howard with Beech, Donna. *The Heartmath Solution*. United States: HarperSanFrancisco a division of HarperCollins Publishers, Inc. 1999. p.140 references: LeDoux, J. E., Emotional memory systems in the brain. *Behavioural Brain Research,* 1993:58 (1-2): 69-79.

[48] Childre, Doc and Martin, Howard with Beech, Donna. *The Heartmath Solution*. United States: HarperSanFrancisco a division of HarperCollins Publishers, Inc. 1999. p.140 references: LeDoux, J. E., *The Emotional Brain: The Mysterious Underpinnings of Emotional Life,* New York: Simon & Schuster, 1996.

[49] Childre, Doc and Martin, Howard with Beech, Donna. *The Heartmath Solution*. United States: HarperSanFrancisco a division of HarperCollins Publishers, Inc. 1999. p.140 references: LeDoux, J. E., Emotional memory systems in the brain. *Behavioural Brain Research,* 1993:58 (1-2): 69-79.

[50] Childre, Doc and Martin, Howard with Beech, Donna. *The Heartmath Solution*. United States: HarperSanFrancisco a division of HarperCollins Publishers, Inc. 1999. p. xv.

[51] Childre, Doc and Martin, Howard with Beech, Donna. *The Heartmath Solution*. United States: HarperSanFrancisco a division of HarperCollins Publishers, Inc. 1999. p.140 references: Pribram, K. H. *Brain and Perception: Holonomy and Structure in Figural Processing.* NJ: Lawrence Erlbaum Associates, 1991.

[52] Childre, Doc and Martin, Howard with Beech, Donna. *The Heartmath Solution*. United States: HarperSanFrancisco a division of HarperCollins Publishers, Inc. 1999. p.140.

[53] Childre, Doc and Martin, Howard with Beech, Donna. *The Heartmath Solution*. United States: HarperSanFrancisco a division of HarperCollins Publishers, Inc. 1999. p.10.

[54] Childre, Doc and Martin, Howard with Beech, Donna. *The Heartmath Solution*. United States: HarperSanFrancisco a division of HarperCollins Publishers, Inc. 1999. p.140 references: Oppenheimer, S., and Hopkins, D. Suprabulbar neuronal regulation of the heart. In: Armour, J.A., and Ardell, J. L., eds. Neurocardiology,. New York: Oxford University Press, 1994;309-341.

[55] Childre, Doc and Martin, Howard with Beech, Donna. *The Heartmath Solution*. United States: HarperSanFrancisco a division of HarperCollins Publishers, Inc. 1999. pp. 7-8.

[56] Childre, Doc and Martin, Howard with Beech, Donna. *The Heartmath Solution*. United States: HarperSanFrancisco a division of HarperCollins Publishers, Inc. 1999. p. 9.

[57] Childre, Doc and Martin, Howard with Beech, Donna. *The Heartmath Solution*. United States: HarperSanFrancisco a division of HarperCollins Publishers, Inc. 1999. p. 9.

[58] Childre, Doc and Martin, Howard with Beech, Donna. *The Heartmath Solution*. United States: HarperSanFrancisco a division of HarperCollins Publishers, Inc. 1999. p. 9.

[59] Childre, Doc and Martin, Howard with Beech, Donna. *The Heartmath Solution*. United States: HarperSanFrancisco a division of HarperCollins Publishers, Inc. 1999. pp. 10-11. references: (a) Lacey, J., and Lacey, B. Some autonomic-central nervous system interrelationships. In: Balck, P., *Physiological Correlates of Emotion*. New York: Academic Press, 1970: 205-227. (b) Frysinger, R. C., and Harper, R. M. Cardiac and respiratory correlations with unit discharge in epileptic human temporal lobe. *Epilepsia*. 1990; 31(2): 162-171, (c) Schandry, R., Sparrer,, B., and Weitkunat, R. From the heart to the brain: a study of heartbeat contingent scalp potentials. *International Journal of Neuroscience*. 1986;30:261-275. (d) McCraty,R., Tiller, W. A. and Atkinson, M. Head-heart entrainment: A preliminary survey. In: *Proceedings of the Brain-Mind Applied Neurophsiology EEG Neurofeedback Meeting*. Key West, Fl, 1996.

[60] Childre, Doc and Martin, Howard with Beech, Donna. *The Heartmath Solution*. United States: HarperSanFrancisco a division of HarperCollins Publishers, Inc. 1999. p 11 references: (a) Frysinger, R. C., and Harper, R. M. Cardiac and respiratory correlations with unit discharge in epileptic human temporal lobe. *Epilepsia*. 1990; 31(2): 162-171, (b) Schandry, R., Sparrer,, B., and Weitkunat, R. From the heart to the brain: a study of heartbeat contingent scalp potentials. *International Journal of Neuroscience*. 1986;30:261-275. (c) McCraty,R., Tiller, W. A. and Atkinson, M. Head-heart entrainment: A preliminary survey. In: *Proceedings of the Brain-Mind Applied Neurophsiology EEG Neurofeedback Meeting*. Key West, Fl, 1996.

[61] Childre, Doc and Martin, Howard with Beech, Donna. *The Heartmath Solution*. United States: HarperSanFrancisco a division of HarperCollins Publishers, Inc. 1999. pp. 28-29 references: McCraty, R., Rozman, D. and Childre, D., eds. *HearthMath: A New Biobehavioral Intervention for Increasing Health and Personal Effectiveness – Increasing Coherence in the Human System* (working title). Amsterdam: Harwood Academic Publishers, 1999 (fall release).

[62] Childre, Doc and Martin, Howard with Beech, Donna. *The Heartmath Solution*. United States: HarperSanFrancisco a division of HarperCollins Publishers, Inc. 1999. p 30 references: Armour, J. Anatomy and function of the intrathoracic neurons regulating the mammalian heart. In: Zucker, I., and Gilmore, J., eds. *Reflex Control of the Circulation*. Doca Raton, FL: CRC Press, 1991:1-37.

[63] Childre, Doc and Martin, Howard with Beech, Donna. *The Heartmath Solution*. United States: HarperSanFrancisco a division of HarperCollins Publishers, Inc. 1999. p. 30 references: McCraty, R., Rozman, D. and Childre, D., eds. *HearthMath: A New Biobehavioral Intervention for Increasing Health and Personal Effectiveness – Increasing Coherence in the Human System* (working title). Amsterdam: Harwood Academic Publishers, 1999 (fall release).

[64] Childre, Doc and Martin, Howard with Beech, Donna. *The Heartmath Solution.* United States: HarperSanFrancisco a division of HarperCollins Publishers, Inc. 1999. p. 13.

[65] Childre, Doc and Martin, Howard with Beech, Donna. *The Heartmath Solution.* United States: HarperSanFrancisco a division of HarperCollins Publishers, Inc. 1999. P. 15 references: (a) McCraty, R., Barrios-Choplin, B., Rosman, D., and others. The impact of a new emotional self-management program on stress, emotions, heart rate variability, DHEA, and cortisol. *Integrative Physiological and Behavioral Science.* 1998;33(2):87-105. (b) Rein, G, Atkinson, M., and McCraty, R. The physiological and psychological effects of compassion and anger. *Journal of Advancement in Medicine.* 1995;8(2):87-105.

[66] Kübler-Ross, Elisabeth and Kessler, David, *Life Lessons.* New York: Scribner, 2000. quote p. 11.

[67] Sun Tzu, Translated by Thomas Cleary. *The Art of War.* Boston: Shambhala Publications, Inc., 1998. p. 1.

[68] Collins, James C. and Porras, Jerry I. *Built to Last* (paperback). New York: HarperBusiness, 1997. table 11.1, p. 225.

[69] Collins, James C. and Porras, Jerry I. *Built to Last* (paperback). New York: HarperBusiness, 1997. table 11.1, p. 225.

[70] Collins, James. *Good To Great—Why Some Companies Make the Leap...and Other's Don't,* New York: Harper Business, 2001. p. 96.

[71] Collins, James. *Good To Great—Why Some Companies Make the Leap...and Other's Don't,* New York: Harper Business, 2001.p. 109.

[72] Collins, James. *Good To Great—Why Some Companies Make the Leap...and Other's Don't,* New York: Harper Business, 2001.pp. 69-70.

[73] Collins, James. *Good To Great—Why Some Companies Make the Leap...and Other's Don't,* New York: Harper Business, 2001.quote p. 70.

[74] Collins, James. *Good To Great—Why Some Companies Make the Leap...and Other's Don't,* New York: Harper Business, 2001. pp. 90-91. Mr. Collins quote is taken from: Isaiah Berlin, *The Hedgehog and the Fox* (Chicago: Elephant Paperbacks, 1993).

[75] Lao Tzu, Translated by John C. H. Wu . *Tao Teh Ching.* Boston: Shambhala Publications, Inc., 1990. Verse 63.

[76] Borg, Marcus. *Jesus and Buddha, The Parallel Sayings.* Berkeley, CA.: Ulysses Press, 1997. p. 15.

[77] Kübler-Ross, Elisabeth and Kessler, David, *Life Lessons.* New York: Scribner, 2000. quote p. 11.

[78] David H. Maister, David H. *Practice What you Preach – What Managers Must Do To Create A High Achievement Culture.* New York: The Free Press, 2001. p. 3.

[79] David H. Maister, David H. *Practice What you Preach – What Managers Must Do To Create A High Achievement Culture.* New York: The Free Press, 2001. p. 1.

[80] David H. Maister, David H. *Practice What you Preach – What Managers Must Do To Create A High Achievement Culture.* New York: The Free Press, 2001. p. 162-163.

[81] David H. Maister, David H. *Practice What you Preach – What Managers Must Do To Create A High Achievement Culture.* New York: The Free Press, 2001. pp. 162-163.

[82] B. F. Skinner, B.F. *Science and Human Behavior.* New York: The Free Press, 1965. p. 9.

[83] B. F. Skinner, B.F. *Science and Human Behavior.* New York: The Free Press, 1965. p. 57.

[84] David H. Maister, David H. *Practice What you Preach – What Managers Must Do To Create A High Achievement Culture.* New York: The Free Press, 2001. pp. 169-170. (Mr. Maister references: Endlich, Lisa. *Goldman Sachs: The Culture of Success.* Knopf, 1999.)

[85] Collins, James C. and Porras, Jerry I. *Built to Last* (paperback). New York: HarperBusiness, 1997. table 11.1, p. 225.

[86] Zukav, Gary. *The Dancing Wu Li Masters—An Overview of the New Physics.* New York: Bantam Books, 1980. p. 52.

[87] Zukav, Gary. *The Dancing Wu Li Masters—An Overview of the New Physics.* New York: Bantam Books, 1980. p. 53

[88] Zukav, Gary. *The Dancing Wu Li Masters—An Overview of the New Physics.* New York: Bantam Books, 1980. p. 54.

[89] Zukav, Gary. *The Dancing Wu Li Masters—An Overview of the New Physics.* New York: Bantam Books, 1980. p. 93.

[90] Zukav, Gary. *The Dancing Wu Li Masters—An Overview of the New Physics.* New York: Bantam Books, 1980. p. 65.

[91] Zukav, Gary. *The Dancing Wu Li Masters—An Overview of the New Physics.* New York: Bantam Books, 1980. p. 93.

[92] Zukav, Gary. *The Dancing Wu Li Masters—An Overview of the New Physics.* New York: Bantam Books, 1980. p. 97.

[93] Bodanis, David. $E=MC^2$, *A Biography of the World's Most Famous Equation.* New York: Walker & Company, 2000. History of the atomic bomb description derived from pp. 117-133.

[94] Zukav, Gary. *The Dancing Wu Li Masters—An Overview of the New Physics.* New York: Bantam Books, 1980. p. 112.

[95] Morris, Betsy. *Tearing up the Jack Welch playbook*. Fortune. 2006. http://money.cnn.com/2006/07/10/magazines/fortune/rule4.fortune/index.htm (Retrieved 2010-08-12). Ms. Morris makes these statements about Six Sigma with the reference "according to an analysis by Charles Holland of consulting firm Qualpro"

[96] Rath, Tom and Clifton, Donald O. *How Full is Your Bucket?—Positive Strategies for Work and Life*. New York: Callup Press, 2004. p. 39.

[97] Adeline Yen Mah, *Watching the Tree*. New York: Broadway Books, 2001, p. 156.

[98] Zukav, Gary. *The Dancing Wu Li Masters—An Overview of the New Physics*. New York: Bantam Books, 1980. p. 298.

[99] Braden, Gregg. *The Divine Matrix—Bridging Time, Space, Miracles, and Belief*. California: Hay House, Inc., 2007. pp. 46-49. Gregg Braden describes experiments conducted by the Army and Dr. Cleve Backster.

[100] Halberstam, Yitta and Leventhal, Judith. *Small Miracles—Extraordinary Coincidences from Everyday Life*. Holbrook, MA: Adams Media Corporation, 1997. pp. 6-7.

[101] Halberstam, Yitta and Leventhal, Judith. *Small Miracles II—Hardwarming Gifts of Extraordinary Coincidences*. Holbrook, MA: Adams Media Corporation, 1998. pp. 71-74.

[102] Halberstam, Yitta and Leventhal, Judith. *Small Miracles—Extraordinary Coincidences from Everyday Life*. Holbrook, MA: Adams Media Corporation, 1997. pp. 25-26.

[103] Brinkley, Dannion with Perry, Paul. *Saved by the Light*, New York: Villard Books, 1994. pp. 10-14.

[104] Brinkley, Dannion with Perry, Paul. *Saved by the Light*, New York: Villard Books, 1994. pp. 16-17.

[105] Brinkley, Dannion with Perry, Paul. *Saved by the Light*, New York: Villard Books, 1994. pp. 18-19.

[106] Brinkley, Dannion with Perry, Paul. *Saved by the Light*, New York: Villard Books, 1994. p. 152.

Notes

Notes

Notes

About the Author

Gabriel Lawson began volunteering at hospice in 1997. He has worked in high-tech corporate America serving as an Executive Director, Vice President, and Senior Vice President in the broadcasting, computer storage, ecommerce, and avionics industries.

A leader in human process improvement, Gabriel implements emotional intelligence principles at both the individual and organizational level.

He lives in Colorado with his wonderful wife, Rebeccea.

For contact information, visit his website at http://www.gabriellawson.com.